CASSIAN'S PRAYER

FOR THE 21ST CENTURY

CASSIAN'S PRAYER

FOR THE 21ST CENTURY

Second Edition

BY

JOHN J. LEVKO, S.J.

SCRANTON: THE UNIVERSITY OF SCRANTON PRESS

Library of Congress Cataloging-in-Publication Data

Levko, John J., 1942-
Cassian's prayer for the 21st century / by John J. Levko.
p.m.
Includes bibliographical references and index.
ISBN 0-940866-95-1 (pbk.)
1. Cassian, John, ca. 360-ca. 435–Contributions in doctrine of prayer. 2.
Prayer–Christianity–History of doctrines–Early church, ca. 30-600. I. Title.

BV207 .L48 2000
248.3'2'092–dc21   00-051879

Distribution:

The University of Scranton Press
Chicago Distribution Center
11030 South Langley
Chicago IL 60628

DEDICATION:

**With Heartfelt Gratitude
To My Beloved Parents,
John and Mary,
Who Made this Possible.**

CONTENTS

PREFACE

This study grew out of my work in the pastoral/retreat ministry in the United States as a Byzantine Jesuit. It was enriched by my research at the Center for Eastern Christian Studies (CECS) of the University of Scranton and the Pontifical Oriental Institute in Rome. I write as an Eastern Christian whose entire spiritual life, while immersed in American society, has been nurtured by the Christian East. In any consumer-oriented society preoccupied with the drive toward perfection and bombarded with hundreds of daily advertisements pushing the limits of ethically acceptable taste, we often find it difficult to transfer this drive to the spiritual realm, even when there exists a desire to do so. As the new millennium dawns, a growing number of people are looking for and in need of a sense of spiritual life, a life of prayer. John Cassian answers that need. While he writes primarily for the monastic life, Cassian's treatment of prayer is universal. His *Conferences* constitute a manual of perfection; a guide for those called to seek the ultimate end, which is eternal life. He is trying to reform Gallican monasticism along Egyptian lines and the structure for progress in prayer that he outlines was woven into the structure of monastic life in the West.

Prayer is the central ingredient for Cassian in any spiritual journey. It is not so much an activity as a state. In fact, the monastic life equals a life of prayer where the only perfection that matters is the inward "state" of the soul. Spiritual growth is intimately connected with prayer and the continual meditation upon Holy Scripture. Prayer acts as the foundation for all other ingredients in the spiritual journey from acquisition of virtues to the highest levels of contemplation.

Whether it is a journey in prayer from "lukewarmness to steadfastness" or "solitude to openness," Cassian's thought centers primarily upon the inner struggle between flesh and spirit. The "pure" life is seen as real preparation for pure prayer where growth in the virtues leads to purity of heart by means of prayer and hence in the gradual transformation into a greater image and likeness of God. The interior transformation through image and likeness in the spiritual struggle is effected, shaped, and nurtured in discerned growth through prayer where it is supported by memory of Scripture, discernment, and the example of others.

Cassian is concerned to show that sin can be destroyed through prayer by discernment, spiritual direction, and self-control. He finds models for prayer in the lives of the Desert Fathers and his journey in prayer nurtured many spiritual writers, including Ignatius of Loyola. On no point has Cassian so faithfully reported the teaching of these Fathers as on the goal of the ascetical life and its development within the context of a growing life of prayer.

While it is not an exegetical analysis of Cassian's works, this study is a synthesis of one of his most practical and important topics, that of prayer. The purpose of the study is to highlight the importance and relevance of Cassian's view of private personal prayer as we enter the 21st century. It is not an exclusively original work so much as an attempt to bring together in synthesis form some of his wisdom from the Christian East concerning prayer. Those readers who are interested in a more developed view of other aspects of Cassian's spiritual theology are encouraged to consult the footnotes and bibliography. I want to thank the publishers of the ecumenical journal *Diakonia* and *St. Vladimir's Theological Quarterly* for permission to use my articles, which appeared in their publications.

Finally, I would like to express words of gratitude to my brothers and sisters in Christ who encouraged me in this work. In addition, appreciation must be expressed to Cardinal Tomáš Špidlík, S.J., and the late Rev. Walter J. Ciszek, S.J., who developed my theoretical and practical understanding of prayer, respectively; to Rev. Joseph L. Quinn, S.J., who made practical, stylistic suggestions concerning parts of the manuscript; and to Rev. Richard W. Rousseau, S.J., and Patricia A. Mecadon of the University of Scranton Press for making the production of this book a reality.

HISTORICAL PERSPECTIVE

John Cassian (ca. 360–435) was born most probably in the Roman province of Scythia Minor, what is now called Romania, modern Dobrudja.[1] It was a time of passionate doctrinal involvement, with all the great questions concerning the relationships first within the Trinity and then between the human and divine natures of Christ coming under increasingly rigorous scrutiny.[2]

In his early years Cassian traveled to the Holy Land and joined a monastery in Bethlehem; later he traveled to Egypt with a friend, Germanus. He remained in Egypt until about 399 and must have met Evagrius[3] while there. While in Constantinople he was ordained a deacon and became a supporter of John Chrysostom.[4] Around the year 405, Cassian traveled west and eventually to Rome before going on to the south of Gaul, where he would share what he saw and learned in the East "to inspire an authentic monastic mind."[5] The travels of Cassian, especially throughout Egypt, allowed him to experience the possibilities and also the limitations of monastic life. It was from these experiences that, as Chadwick says, he began "to create out of the diversity of Egyptian ideas a coherent scheme of spirituality."[6]

He became a priest and founded two monasteries near Marseilles around the year 415: one for men (St. Victor's) and the other for women (Holy Savior's). As Guy says,[7]

> Cassian is said to have had the intention of reproducing the lessons that he received from his Egyptian masters in adapting them to the exigencies of life in the south of Gaul. In reality, he rethought and systematized this teaching, not without enriching it with abundant readings.

---

[1] *John Cassian*, 2nd ed., by Owen Chadwick, Cambridge University Press, 1968, p. 9.

[2] *John Cassian: Conferences*, trans. & pref. by Colm Luibheid, Paulist Press, 1985, p. xi.

[3] Chadwick, *op. cit.*, p. 26.

[4] *Ibid.*, pp. 30–31.

[5] *"Jean Cassien, historien du monachisme égyptien?"* by Jean-Claude Guy, S.J., SP 8 (1966), 372.

[6] Luibheid, *op. cit.*, p. 2.

[7] *"Ecriture Sainte: dans le monachisme,"* DSAM 4,1: 163–164.

A reasonable approximation of the time period by which Cassian finished all three of his works is 425 to 430.[8] In his two most important works, the *Institutes* and *Conferences*, he tried to summarize all the spiritual teaching he had received in Egypt by giving testimony on the monastic life in lower Egypt in the 4th century. First, his intention in the *Institutes* was to provide[9]

> the customs of the monasteries which have been observed through-
> out Egypt and Palestine, as they were there delivered to us by the
> Fathers; not looking for graceful speech . . . but wanting the simple
> life of holy men to be told in simple language to the brethren in your
> new monastery.

While the *Institutes* tended to give the outer form of coenobitic life and its ascesis in the remedies for the eight principal vices, the *Conferences*, Cassian's second work, highlighted the progress from the exterior to the interior man: they showed the Egyptian ideal of inner ascent to perfection. Finally, in order to counter the doctrinal errors attributed to Nestorius, Cassian wrote *De Incarnatione*.

Our work here is specifically concerned with Cassian's concept of prayer. In order to appreciate his understanding and development of prayer, it will be useful to ascertain what has been done in the recent past.

---

[8] Chadwick, *op. cit.*, p. 39.

[9] *Inst.*, preface.

RECENT AUTHORS

Among the many recent authors who have included some aspect of Cassian's concept of prayer in their work, the most well known are probably Salvatore Marsili, Jean-Claude Guy, Owen Chadwick, and Columba Stewart. While there are other authors who have studied the topic of prayer in Cassian, none has attempted a general in-depth synthesis.

Salvatore Marsili's work, *Giovanni Cassiano ed Evagrio Pontico*, considers the relation between charity and contemplation; he is basically concerned with an analysis of the supreme grade of prayer (or contemplation) in Cassian's work. While he uses the "Our Father" as an example of the method and form of prayer, Marsili indicates[10] that "it is not his intent to research all the possible aspects that prayer can assume." He points out that pure prayer (*proseuche*) is often identified by Cassian with contemplation. According to Marsili, it is by growing toward *apatheia* and charity that the monk will be at the door of contemplation;[11] common to both Evagrius and Cassian is that perfect purity and contemplation are graces and gifts of the Lord.[12] In explaining the fourfold[13] nature of prayer from 1 Tim. 2:1–2, Cassian begins at the stage of thanksgiving to refer to the contemplative phase, which at its roots is always under the influence of divine inspiration.[14] In fact, for Marsili[15] it is thanksgiving, *gratiarum actio*, which derives from contemplation *futurorum bonorum*.

Among his many works concerning Cassian, Jean-Claude Guy has probably the best introduction to him in a work entitled *Jean Cassien: Vie et doctrine spirituelle*. It deals with a broad analysis of the spiritual life of Cassian quoting both *Institutes* and *Conferences* but only provides a brief discussion of one of Cassian's two conferences on prayer, and

---

[10] *"Giovanni Cassiano ed Evagrio Pontico: Dottrina sulla carita e contemplatione"* by Salvatore Marsili, O.S.B., SA, Fasciculus V. Romae: Herder, 1936, p. 145.

[11] *Ibid.*, p. 131. See also *Conf.* 10:9.

[12] *Ibid.*, p. 142.

[13] Cf. *Conf.* 9:9, 9:15. Supplication (*obsecratio*), prayer (*oratio*), intercession (*postulatio*), and thanksgiving (*gratiarum actio*).

[14] Marsili, *op. cit.*, p. 30.

[15] *Ibid.*, p. 62; note *Conf.* 9:16.

even this is only a particular analysis of one aspect of prayer, the prayer of fire.[16]

While explaining Cassian's conception of the monk's spiritual journey, Guy develops his subject's doctrine concerning the use of Holy Scripture.[17] Even though he briefly mentions the importance of spiritual discernment and humility in the journey toward monastic perfection,[18] Guy does not develop the relationship between prayer and the use of Scripture. Also, he does not develop the relationship of Scripture to spiritual discernment, humility and patience, and the growth process into the image and likeness of God.

According to Marsili,[19] Cassian intended to transmit principally Egyptian monastic doctrine from the beginning. However, Guy not only questions the historical objectivity of Cassian's information,[20] but also points out that "Cassian does not appear as a true witness of Egyptian monastic life."[21] Indeed, Guy warns against "a too facile credulity towards Cassian as an historian."[22] Nevertheless, for Guy this does not compromise Cassian's position on prayer, since as Guy admits, "Cassian has nothing to do with being an historian. He is a theoretician of spiritual life, and a theoretician of an outstanding originality and depth."[23] I myself am less negative than Guy and assert that the basic material Cassian used was the tradition of desert teaching, and that his works filtered these early ideals for use in the West. In fact, on no point has Cassian so faithfully reported the teaching of the Desert Fathers as on the development of the ascetical life within the context of a growing life of prayer.

Owen Chadwick's primary work, entitled *John Cassian*,[24] is probably the best-documented survey in English of the life and work of Cassian. In his second chapter, entitled "The Monastery," Chadwick very ably discusses the text of the *Institutes* and the rule of the

---

[16] *Jean Cassien: Vie et doctrine spirituelle* by Jean-Claude Guy, S.J., Paris, 1961, p. 55.

[17] *Ibid.*, p. 43

[18] *Ibid.*, pp. 49–52.

[19] Marsili, *op. cit.*, p. 78.

[20] *"Jean Cassien, historien du monachisme égyptien?"* by Jean-Claude Guy, S.J., SP 8 (1966), 366, 372.

[21] *Ibid.*, p. 369.

[22] *Ibid.*, p. 371.

[23] *Ibid.*, p. 372.

[24] Chadwick, *op. cit.*

monastery. Here he does an excellent job of discussing the offices of prayer. While he questions the historical objectivity and authenticity of several of Cassian's statements concerning prayer practices,[25] Chadwick concludes that "Cassian is not a reporter or transmitter of historical detail and facts but a formulator of spirituality that rested upon tradition and experience."[26] It is in the third chapter, entitled "The Journey of the Soul," that Chadwick discusses prayer itself. He provides a very brief and at times a superficial sketch of Cassian's two conferences on prayer. He states[27] that "Cassian believed that the 'empty mind' might be demonic. The thoughts were not to be expelled but controlled."

Columba Stewart's book *Cassian the Monk* is a well-written but limited study of the life, monastic writings, and spiritual theology of Cassian in seven chapters, the last three of which are concerned with Cassian's doctrine of prayer. As Stewart admits,[28] "important topics such as the discernment of thoughts, Cassian's consideration of the traditional eight principal faults and many other aspects of his ascetical theology receive little direct attention in this study." This is a concern given the desire of Stewart to represent "Cassian's understanding of human development"[29] and the percentage of material that Stewart devotes to Cassian's doctrine of prayer and the interrelatedness of these omitted topics with prayer. There is a direct relationship for Cassian of growth in prayer to *discretio* and conforming to the image of God,[30] yet Stewart is hesitant at best in referencing any such relationship.

Stewart mentions the concept of "elder" and highlights the importance of Cassian's "integrative view of the human person"[31] yet fails to adequately reference the significance of spiritual direction, which is of primary importance in this integration process. In order to facilitate the journey in prayer, Cassian insists upon the importance of a spiritual

---

[25] *Ibid.*, pp. 49–50, 58–59.

[26] *A Descriptive Presentation on John Cassian and His Treatise on Prayer: The Relationship of Virtue and Prayer* by Michael J. Jennett, Dissertation ad Lauream in Facultate S. Theologiae Apud Pontificiam Universitatem S. Thomae de Urbe, Roma, 1981, p. 56.

[27] Chadwick, *op. cit.*, p. 104.

[28] *Cassian the Monk* by Columba Stewart, New York, Oxford University Press, 1998, p. vii.

[29] *Ibid.*, p. viii.

[30] Cf. *Conf.* 10:6.

[31] *Ibid.*, p. 132.

father (elder or guide) who intercedes and mediates God's grace for the directee. It's here that discernment and spiritual direction for Cassian interconnect in each Christian life. As discernment is situated in the context of prayer, so too Cassian sees prayer as undergirding spiritual direction, especially in the early stages of the spiritual journey, for the soul matures in prayer through discernment. Probably more basic than this last shortcoming, especially with regard to Cassian's description of prayer, is the fact that although he does mention it in several places,[32] Stewart does not elaborate on the importance for Cassian of "disposition" or "state" of prayer. The inner struggle to develop a spiritual turn to one's memory was gradual for Cassian and effected a spiritual transformation, which in turn helped to establish a prayerful disposition. For Cassian the interior transformation through image and likeness[33] in the spiritual struggle is dynamic and personal, and is effected and nurtured through prayer. He insisted upon both the struggle and God's grace which, as Chadwick said, was "presupposed, not omitted."[34]

While each of these four authors presents a valuable, but limited, study of Cassian's concept of prayer, our work endeavors to provide a synthesis of the meaning, practice, disposition, and effects of Cassian's prayer leading up to and including the prayer of fire. The intimate connection between progress in prayer and spiritual growth for Cassian is studied as well as the relationship of prayer to *discretio* and conforming to the image of God. We extend the work of Marsili and Guy by studying the relationship of Scripture to spiritual discernment, humility, and patience as well as the relatedness of Scripture to the inner struggle, spiritual growth, and prayer. We enhance the work of Chadwick and Stewart by showing the importance for Cassian of self-control, internal disposition, discernment, and spiritual direction in the journey of prayer.

---

[32] *Ibid.*, note 35, p. 31.

[33] Gen. 1:26–27.

[34] Chadwick, *op.cit.*, p. 116; see *Conf.* 4:5. For a discussion of Cassian and the Pelagian/semi-Pelagian questions see Chadwick, *op.cit.*, pp. 19–20, 113–136 and Stewart, *op.cit.*, pp. 19–22, 77–81.

CHAPTER 1

PRAYER

As we enter the 21st century, the struggle for our consumer-oriented attention continues to grow exponentially. Advertisers troll constantly with increased target marketing where the practical concern is "what we like—what we buy—what we go back and buy again." But, we encounter this constant call to practicality in every walk of life, even in the spiritual. The words of John Cassian speak to this call, especially in prayer.

1. *WHAT IS PRAYER FOR CASSIAN?*

Prayer for the blessed Antony is seen as a life of conflict in which evil forces are encountered and defeated, for "as Scripture says, let us keep our heart in all watchfulness (Prov. 4:23). For we have terrible and villainous enemies—the evil demons, and our contending is against these."[1] As Antony admits, "we need not fear their suggestions, for by prayer and fasting and by faith in the Lord they are brought down immediately."[2] Faith in the Lord is for Antony the desire to allow the Word of God and His will to shape each moment of our lives through His Spirit. Origen links prayer and faith,[3] but also highlights the importance of the internal disposition before and during prayer for "the person who is about to come to prayer should withdraw for a little and prepare himself, and so become more attentive and active for the whole of his prayer."[4]

---

[1] Robert C. Gregg, *Athanasius, The Life of Antony and the Letter to Marcellinus*, translation and introduction, Paulist Press, New York, 1980, p. 47. See *Vita Antonii*, 21.

[2] *Ibid.*, p. 48; *Vita*, 23; also, *Vita*, 4, 5, 27, 30, 40, 47.

[3] Origen, *On Prayer*, 11:5, 12:1. See *Origen*, with trans. & intro. by Rowan A. Greer, The Classics of Western Spirituality Series, Paulist Press, New York, 1979.

[4] *Ibid.*, 31:2.

Among the many definitions of prayer given throughout the ages, probably the three best known in the Christian tradition, as highlighted by Tomáš Špidlík, are the following:[5]

> (1) asking God for what is fitting; (2) an ascent of the spirit to God; (3) the spirit's colloquy with God. John of Damascus unified the first and the second definition: "Prayer is an ascent of the mind to God, or the asking God for things which are fitting,"[6] a formula borrowed by many others.[7]

Prayer is, in one sense, the filial expression of one's desires for self and others to the heavenly Father from whom come all good things, natural or supernatural. In a wider sense, it is the ascent of the mind to God.

For Cassian, prayer is a comprehensive term composed of a fourfold nature in which he presents four kinds of prayer[8] according to the fourfold divisions[9] listed by St. Paul in 1 Tim. 2:1. He certainly echoes the dynamic, personal thought of Evagrius, who says that prayer is a state of continual recollection,[10] "the fruit of joy and of thanksgiving" and "the exclusion of sadness and despondency."[11] Although prayer is addressed to God,[12] Cassian sees Jesus as the divine teacher of prayer and insists that He is our example for prayer.[13] For Cassian, we ought to ask in faith-filled confidence for only those things which are

---

[5] SHI, pp. 308–309.

[6] *De fide orthodoxa* 3.24; PG 94:1089C.

[7] Thomas Aquinas, *Summa Theologiae* II–II. 83. 1c; *Expositio in epistolam beati Pauli ad Colossenses*, 1.3.

[8] *Conf.* 9:9. For the English translation of Cassian's texts, see that of Edgar Gibson in "The Works of John Cassian," NPNF, Vol. XI, 2nd series (Eerdmans Publ. Co., 1964). The following may also be consulted: (1) Boniface Ramsey in John Cassian: *The Conferences*, ACW 57 (1997) and *John Cassian: The Institutes*, ACW 58 (2000), (2) Colm Luibheid in *John Cassian: Conferences*, Paulist Press, New York, 1985, and (3) Owen Chadwick in *Western Asceticism*, Library of Christian Classics, The Westminster Press, Philadelphia, Vol. XII, 1958.

[9] *Deesis* (supplication), *proseuche* (prayer), *enteuxis* (intercession), *eucharistia* (thanksgiving).

[10] *Evagrius Ponticus: The Praktikos & Chapters on Prayer*, trans. by John Eudes Bamberger, OCSO, CSS 4, Cistercian Publ., 1981, *Prayer*, 3, 52, 102.

[11] *Ibid.*, 15–16.

[12] *Conf.* 9:12.

[13] *Ibid.*, 10:6.

contained in the limits of the Lord's Prayer,[14] for allowing God's will to come to perfection in our lives "through prayer" is of the highest priority for him: "following the example of the Lord, we should end all our prayers like His, adding to all our petitions the words 'However, not as I wish, but as you wish.'"[15]

WHEN IS PRAYER HEARD?

In a world often obsessed with demonstrating confidence in nearly every walk of life, we often forget that confidence plays an important role in the spiritual life, especially during the journey in prayer. Many of the early Christian spiritual writers[16] refer to confidence, but few develop such a practical view as Cassian, who understands it as being part of the internal disposition of true prayer. It is prayer in faith-filled confidence[17] which is heard by God. Cassian understands confidence as part of the internal disposition which "flows from purity of conscience" and is always tempered by humility.[18] Faith-filled confidence in a prayerful disposition gradually allows one to "not care about the quantity of verses, but about the intelligence of the mind; aiming with all their might at this: 'I will sing with the spirit: I will sing also with the understanding' (1 Cor. 14:15),"[19] for if

> . . . while we are praying, no hesitation intervenes and breaks down the confidence of our petition by a sort of despair, but we feel that by pouring forth our prayer we have obtained what we are asking for, we have no doubt that *our prayers have effectually reached God.*[20]

---

[14] *Ibid.*, 9:24.

[15] *Ibid.*, 9:18–20, 24, 34.

[16] Cf. Origen, *On Prayer* 9:1, 10:1, 19:1, 30:1; Evagrius, *Praktikos* 89, *Prayer* 80, 92, 94. As Origen states: "God delivers us from the Evil One not when the Enemy who wrestles against us (Eph. 6:11–12) has in no way attacked us through any of his crafts and any of the servants of his will, but when we are gaining the victory *with courage* by standing firm against what happens to us" (*On Prayer*, 30:1; emphasis mine). According to Evagrius, "if you pray in all truth you will come upon a deep sense of confidence (*Prayer*, 80) . . . pray with tears and your request will find a hearing. Nothing so gratifies the Lord as supplication offered in the midst of tears" (*Prayer*, 6).

[17] *Conf.* 9:32.

[18] *Ibid.*, 9:33.

[19] *Inst.* 2:11.

[20] *Conf.* 9:32. Emphasis mine. Also, see 9:34 and 1 Jn. 5:14.

Prayer in faith-filled confidence is intimately connected for Cassian with developing a God-centered internal disposition[21] based on the virtues.

For Cassian, it is nurturing the experience of humility by means of prayer which allows one to grow in spiritual self-knowledge through discernment.[22] It is the confidence resulting from this experience which Cassian recognizes besides grace as helping growth in discernment. In his portrait of a true spiritual guide, Cassian insists on the virtue of humility, which is necessary for discernment. A simple discussion with a spiritual guide can lead to growth in humility, peace in one's prayer life, and inner freedom from "confession."[23] Cassian implies a relationship between being cleansed or set free from sin by the daily grace of Christ and prayer to Christ.[24] He highlights the importance of a "spiritually minded person who knows how to heal"[25] and realizes that the cleaning of a wound is a prerequisite for its healing. How much more important is this for "invisible wounds," those wounds for which there are no exterior marks? Cassian knows that helping to heal the afflictions of the body and soul is the practice of fasting, not only from foods, which affect the body, but more importantly, fasting as an external manifestation of prayer.

2. INCESSANT PRAYER

Cassian places great value not only on brevity in prayer but also on frequency and repetition. Prayer is dynamically cyclic for him. It is prompted by Holy Scripture, which is taken in, allowed to affect the heart, and made one's own only to be fulfilled in one's daily life. The spiritual journey for Cassian is a gradual conforming to the image of

---

[21] For Cassian, growth in prayer always allows for growth toward an internal absorption, where our Lord brings the soul back within the "eyes of the heart" (*Conf.* 3:7, 10:6, and *Inst.* 5:34) and the soul sees itself illuminated by celestial light.

[22] *Conf.* 2:10.

[23] *Ibid.*, 2:11; the "confession" mentioned here is not a sacramental act as in our daily and strict sense, but an ascetical means of spiritual help in one's aspiration for spiritual perfection, especially in prayer.

[24] *Ibid.*, 23:15; see also *De Incarn.*, 7:1. Cassian mentions prayer to Jesus in the context of calling upon the name of Christ to help us transform our interior life through His Spirit: *Conf.* 15:3, 5, 7.

[25] *Ibid.*, 2:11.

God,[26] which is the concomitant result of continual recollection of God and incessant prayer.

In order to help battle possible temptations to prevent the revealing of all secrets of the heart to a spiritual guide, Cassian highlights the value of constant prayer in the heart to help develop "an impregnable wall for all who are laboring under the attacks of demons."[27] The monastic soul is one completely striving toward perfect purity of heart and incessant prayer; it is to become a living and constant prayer that confesses the indispensability of God's grace in overcoming temptation. For Cassian, the practice of continual prayer helps to keep the monk aware of God's presence.

The theme of unceasing prayer for Cassian is important to the monastic life[28] and the objective of all perfection:

> This then ought to be the destination of the solitary, this should be all his aim that it may be vouchsafed to him to possess even in the body an image of future bliss, and that he may begin in this world to have a foretaste of a sort of earnest of that celestial life and glory. This, I say, is the end of all perfection, that the mind, purged from all carnal desires, may be daily lifted towards spiritual things, until the whole life and all the thoughts of the heart *become one continuous prayer.*[29]

In this text Cassian highlights a sense of unity between the ideal of perfection in the spiritual life and the oneness with God created by continuous prayer. The structure of the text is framed by Cassian with the verbs "(may) begin," "(may) be lifted (towards)," and "become." Yet it is the ideal of perfection, which provides the deepest meaning for the text, and which Cassian emphasizes by the corresponding significance of the words "destination," "end," and "one" (continuous prayer). The core of the text is contained in the lines "the mind purged from all carnal desires may be lifted towards spiritual things, until the whole life and all the thoughts of the heart become one continuous prayer." The key words here for Cassian are to "become one continuous prayer"; the

---

[26] For Cassian, the interior transformation through image and likeness (Gen. 1:26–27) in the spiritual struggle is dynamic and personal, and is effected and nurtured through prayer.

[27] *Conf.* 10:10.

[28] *Ibid.,* 10:7–11.

[29] *Ibid.,* 10:7. Emphasis mine.

dynamic words "to become" highlight the central idea of the need to "be daily lifted towards" spiritual things. This "becoming" is a spiritual ascent and dynamic change, which Cassian sees as a gradual participation in God. It is a movement upward toward oneness with God, a oneness that is realized in practical terms by growth toward pure prayer.

If we read the Fathers of the desert, we rarely find a discursive treatise on prayer. It is almost impossible to methodize the most intimate stages of assimilation by loving surrender into God. This assimilation means a clinging utterly to God and is based on two principles for Cassian:

> . . . that we should first learn by what meditations God may be grasped and contemplated, and next that we should manage to keep a very firm hold of this topic whatever it is which we do not doubt is the height of all perfection.[30]

These Fathers could give to a disciple a word by which they could be saved, a word that could prepare the groundwork for spiritual growth. Cassian saw the supernatural value of this growth through the *rhema* (word or saying) uttered frequently by the Fathers, as Hausherr says, "presupposed rather than stated explicitly."[31] Spiritual fathers could tell a disciple *how* to fast and make vigils, do penance, cry out for tears and a continued state of compunction, and how to say a prayer, but ultimately they knew that God had to take over eventually, and then it was a matter of personal experience. No one but God could give that experience. As Jesus said: "If anyone loves me he will keep my word, and my Father will love him, and we shall come to him and make our home with him" (Jn. 14:23). Prayer is the awareness of this holy presence, and it is the adoration and completely self-surrendering worship that follows from this awareness. The self-surrendering worship has as a concomitant result the totally integrated union of praying Christians with their Lord, or as Origen says, a union of dispositions and desires about divine things:

> And he prays "constantly" [deeds of virtue or fulfilling the commandments are included as part of prayer] who unites prayer with

---

[30] *Ibid.*, 10:8.

[31] *Spiritual Direction in the Early Christian East* by Irénée Hausherr, CSS 116, Cistercian Publications, Kalamazoo, Michigan, 1990, p. 257.

the deeds required and right deeds with prayer. For the only way we can accept the command to "pray constantly" (1 Thess. 5:17) as referring to a real possibility is by saying that the entire life of the saint taken as a whole is a single great prayer.[32]

Cassian bears witness to his dependence on the doctrine of Origen by saying that:

> When the soul has been established in such a peaceful condition, and has been freed from the meshes of all carnal desires, and the purpose of the heart has been steadily fixed on that which is the only highest good, he will then fulfill this Apostolic precept: "Pray without ceasing" (1 Thess. 5:17).[33]

This dependence is only highlighted by a developed passage from Evagrius:

> We have received no command to work and to pass the night in vigils and to fast constantly. However, we do have the obligation to pray without ceasing. Although the body, due to its weakness, does not suffice for such labors as these, which are calculated to restore health to the passionate part of the soul, these practices do require the body for their performance. But prayer makes the spirit strong and pure for combat since by its very nature the spirit is made to pray. Moreover, prayer even fights without the aid of the body on behalf of the other powers of the soul.[34]

Cassian certainly follows Evagrius, and of course Origen, in calling for unceasing prayer. He is practical and understands that growth toward the realization of incessant prayer is gradual and includes two important elements which are not mutually exclusive: (1) internal union with God: with and without words, and (2) the value of short prayer.

INTERNAL UNION WITH GOD: WITH AND WITHOUT WORDS

In order to understand better Cassian's view of incessant prayer in the spiritual journey toward internal union with God, there is a need to appreciate the importance of keeping one's heart still. As Cassian says:

---

[32] Origen, *On Prayer*, 12:2.

[33] *Conf.* 9:6.

[34] Bamberger, *op. cit.*, p. 29; *Praktikos*, 49.

There are three things that make a shifting heart steadfast, watchings, meditation, and prayer, diligence in which and constant attention will produce steadfast firmness of mind. But this cannot be secured in any other way unless all cares and anxieties of this present life have been first got rid of by indefatigable persistence in work dedicated not to avarice but to the sacred uses of the monastery, that we may thus be able to fulfill the Apostle's command: "Pray without ceasing" (1 Thess. 5:17).[35]

To "pray always" and "watch and pray" were watchwords of the early Church. Evagrius makes clear that "we do have the obligation to pray without ceasing."[36] For Cassian, unceasing prayer helps to minimize distractions as well as aids in liberating the monk from the rule of limited prayer whether collective or obligatory. Cassian states:

. . . that which is continuously offered is more than what is rendered at intervals of time; and more acceptable as a free gift than the duties which are performed by the compulsion of a rule: as David for this rejoices somewhat exultingly when he says, "Freely will I sacrifice unto Thee"; and, "Let the free will offerings of my mouth be pleasing to Thee, O Lord" (Ps. 53:8; 118:108).[37]

Indeed, as Evagrius admits, "Happy is the spirit which, praying without distraction, goes on increasing its desire for God."[38] According to A. G. Wathen,

In order to see the significance in prayer of stability of the soul it is necessary to have some idea of Cassian's thought regarding idle talk, chattering and gossip. The monk is to avoid such talk, which implies he is to keep silent at times. In Cassian's mind silence could be both a virtue and a vice.[39]

To minimize the frequency of idle talk, Cassian encourages the monk to repeat by heart some psalm or passage of Scripture:

---

[35] *Conf.* 10:14.

[36] *Praktikos*, 49.

[37] *Inst.* 3:2.

[38] *Chapters on Prayer*, 118.

[39] *Silence* by Ambrose G. Wathen, OSB, CSS 22 (1973) 120.

By repeating by heart some Psalm or passage of Scripture, he gives no opportunity or time for dangerous schemes or evil designs, or even for idle talk, as both mouth and heart are incessantly taken up with spiritual meditations.[40]

Spiritual thoughts will not easily be attained by idle gossip. As Cassian says:

... if we are overcome by sloth or carelessness and spend our time in idle gossip, or are entangled in the cares of this world and unnecessary anxieties, the result will be that a sort of species of tares will spring up, and afford an injurious occupation for our hearts, and as our Lord and Saviour says,[41] wherever the treasure of our works or purpose may be, there also our heart is sure to continue.[42]

In order to minimize an injurious occupation of the heart at "the time of prayer," Cassian highlights the importance of the memory, especially its role in the quality of prayer: ". . . for the mind of man cannot be emptied of all thoughts, and so as long as it is not taken up with spiritual interests, it is sure to be occupied with what it learnt long since."[43] Cassian understands that

What we would be found when at our prayers, that we ought to be *before the time of prayer*. For at the time of its prayers the mind cannot help being affected by its previous condition, and while it is praying, will be either transported to things heavenly, or dragged down to earthly things by those thoughts in which it had been lingering *before* prayer.[44]

"The time of prayer" and "incessant prayer" are not mutually exclusive expressions for Cassian. In fact, the former includes the latter in the growth process. Just as maturing prayer results in tranquillity of heart, growth in prayer is a gradual process and occurs normally little by little. In order to have a pure heart at prayer, Cassian understood the need to avoid idle words, and wanted

---

[40] *Inst.* 2:15.

[41] Cf. Mt. 6:21.

[42] *Conf.* 1:18.

[43] *Ibid.*, 14:13.

[44] *Ibid.*, 10:14. Emphasis mine.

the soul kept free from all conversation and from roving thoughts that thus it may little by little begin to rise to the contemplation of God and to spiritual insight[45] . . . we shall not possibly attain to those more sublime kinds of supplication of which we spoke, unless our mind has been little by little and by degrees raised through the regular course of those intercessions.[46]

In order to grow in purity of heart and hence in prayer,[47] control of the tongue is seen as important by Cassian. Nevertheless, this is not the same as that silence or lack of all verbal communication as best experienced in the desert: ". . . the Abbot Paul had made such progress in purity of heart in the stillness and silence of the desert."[48] The inner discipline of prayer becomes important. Freedom demands inner discipline. To know purity of heart, or true love,[49] is to be free from all attachments.[50] For Cassian, ". . . he is indeed free, who has begun to be led captive by Thee [Lord Jesus]."[51] Cassian relates this freedom to one's ability to feel at peace during prayer with silence, both exterior and interior. As Wathen points out, "silence or the absence of verbal communication between monks is considered both negatively and positively by Cassian . . . there is an undesirable as well as a desirable silence."[52] Cassian reminds us that silence during the journey in prayer is a direct consequence of the Gospel request to pray with the door closed:

Before all things however we ought most carefully to observe the Evangelic precept, which tells us to enter into our chamber and shut the door and pray to our Father, which may be fulfilled by us as follows: We pray within our chamber, when removing our hearts inwardly from the din of all thoughts and anxieties, we disclose our prayers in secret and in closest intercourse to the Lord. We pray with

---

[45] *Ibid.*, 9:3. See Wathen, *op. cit.*, p. 121.

[46] *Ibid.*, 9:16.

[47] *Ibid.*, 7:26, 14:4, 19:10, 24:18.

[48] *Ibid.*, 7:26.

[49] True love, that is, the love of the Son who loves the Father, not out of fear, not out of hope of reward, but for love's sake alone; see Michel Olphe-Galliard, S.J., "*La Pureté de Coeur d'après Cassien*," RAM 17 (1936), 28–60.

[50] Cf. *De Incarn.* 5:15; *Inst.* 4:34–35.

[51] *De Incarn.* 7:1.

[52] Wathen, *op. cit.*, p. 122.

closed doors when *with closed lips and complete silence* we pray to
the searcher not of words but of hearts.[53]

It seems that silence as restraint of speech is a relative good.
Indeed, it can even be bad. Whether it is good or evil depends upon its
motivation. Motivated by vainglory and pride or by anger and dejection,
silence is an evil. But motivated by humility, a desire to listen to
spiritual doctrine or to meditate on Scripture, or to grow toward unceasing prayer, silence is a good and is to be cultivated. Pure prayer can
flourish and grow within this context of silence. Silence can only be
evaluated insofar as it is related to something else. When it is related to
a vice it is evil. When it is related to a virtue it is good. One does not
find any indication that silence is good or evil in itself. It is always
functional for good or for evil.[54]

Silence can be a hindrance to prayer and indeed not desirable, if as
Cassian says,[55] it "denotes not compunction or humility, but pride and
wrath." Nevertheless, there is desirable silence, which is conducive to
prayer. As Cassian admits, when a monk retires to his cell, he

> ... does the work assigned to him in such a way that, by repeating by
> heart some Psalm or passage of Scripture, he gives no opportunity or
> time for dangerous schemes or evil designs, or even for idle talk, as
> both mouth and heart are incessantly taken up with spiritual
> meditation.[56]

Yet, for Cassian, the humility and patience needed to acquire true peace
of heart for prayer are not automatically obtained by external silence:

> ... true patience and tranquillity is neither gained nor retained
> without profound humility of heart: and if it has sprung from this
> source, there will be no need either of the good offices of the cell or
> of the refuge of the desert. For it will seek no external support from
> anything, if it has the internal support of the virtue of humility, and its
> mother and its guardian.[57]

---

[53] *Conf.* 9:35; emphasis mine. See Mt. 6:6.

[54] Wathen, *op. cit.*, pp. 127–128.

[55] *Inst.* 12:27.

[56] *Ibid.*, 2:15.

[57] *Conf.* 18:13.

For true peace of heart, the virtues of humility and patience must be acquired, as Cassian exemplifies in the verse of the Psalmist:

> I said I will take heed to my ways that I offend not with my tongue.
> I set a guard to my mouth when the sinner stood before me. I was
> dumb and was humbled and kept silence from good things.[58]

In the journey of prayer, a state may eventually be reached where words are not necessary. Silence permeates this state—a state, which Cassian says,

> ... transcends all human thoughts, and is distinguished, I will not say
> by any sound of the voice, but by no movement of the tongue, or
> utterance of words, but which the mind *enlightened by the infusion of
> that heavenly light describes in no human and confined language*, but
> pours forth richly as from a copious fountain in an accumulation of
> thoughts, and ineffably utters to God, expressing in the shortest
> possible space of time such great things that the mind when it returns
> to its usual condition cannot easily utter or relate.[59]

There will be times, as Cassian admits, when no words will be able to express one's feeling, especially of compunction:

> ... sometimes the mind hides itself in complete silence within the
> secrets of a profound quiet, so that the amazement of a sudden
> illumination chokes all sounds of words and the overawed spirit either
> keeps all its feelings to itself or loses them and pours forth its desires
> to God with groanings that cannot be uttered.[60]

This certainly echoes the experience of Evagrius who reminds us that "happy is the spirit that attains to complete unconsciousness of all sensible experience at the time of prayer."[61] Certainly, "the purest prayer can indeed be silence. Silence can be prayer; it can be the realization of the monk's goal."[62] Through the words of the blessed Antony,

---

[58] Ps. 38:2–3; see *Inst.* 4:41; *Conf.* 16:26.

[59] *Conf.* 9:25. Emphasis mine.

[60] *Ibid.*, 9:27.

[61] *Chapters on Prayer*, 120.

[62] Wathen, *op. cit.*, p. 126.

Cassian reminds us "that is not . . . a perfect prayer, wherein a monk understands himself and the words which he prays."[63]

In Cassian's journey of perfection in prayer toward internal union with God, prayer with and without words plays a significant role toward the realization of incessant prayer. Growth in unceasing prayer is the concomitant result of the deepening of the inner silence of one's heart.

VALUE OF SHORT PRAYER

In order to grow more fully in the acceptance of what Evagrius calls the obligation to pray without ceasing, Cassian advocates a short prayer formula.[64] Simple prayer consisting of short phrases drawn from Scripture played an important role in the prayer life of the early monks. One of the most frequently used verses was *Deus in adiutorium meum intende*, "O God, come to my aid!"[65] Cassian insists that

> . . . for keeping up continual recollection of God this pious formula is to be ever set before you. "O God, make speed to save me: O Lord, make haste to help me (Ps. 69:2)," for this verse has not unreasonably been picked out from the whole of Scripture for this purpose. For it embraces all the feelings which can be implanted in human nature, and can be fitly and satisfactorily adapted to every condition, and all assaults.[66]

In the eyes of the ancient monks, brevity was a characteristic of authentic prayer, and this in conformity to the Gospel precept where Jesus says: "in your prayers do not babble as the pagans do, for they think that by using many words they will make themselves heard."[67] Cassian coupled this with the element of frequency:

> . . . they think it best for the prayers to be short and offered up very frequently: on the one hand that by so often praying to the Lord we may be able to cleave to Him continually; on the other, that when the

---

[63] *Conf.* 9:31.

[64] *Ibid.*, 10:10.

[65] *Ibid.*; see Ps. 69:2 from Gibson, *op. cit.*, p. 405.

[66] *Ibid.* The relationship between "praying always" and distractions is considered in a paper entitled *"Pray Always: John Cassian on Distractions"* by Kenneth C. Russell, RR 53, 2 (1994), 263–272.

[67] Mt. 6:7.

devil is lying in wait for us, we may by their terse brevity avoid the darts with which he endeavors to wound us especially when we are saying our prayers.[68]

For Evagrius,

the value of prayer is found not merely in its quantity but also in its quality. This is made clear by those two men who entered the temple, and by the saying: "when you pray do not do a lot of empty chattering."[69]

He said that at the time of temptations one was to make use of short and intense prayer.[70] Cassian follows this advice by saying that

. . . we ought to pray often but briefly, lest if we are long about it our crafty foe may succeed in implanting something in our heart. For that is the true sacrifice, as "the sacrifice of God is a broken spirit" (Ps. 50:19). This is the salutary offering, these are pure drink offerings, that is the "sacrifice of righteousness," the "sacrifice of praise," these are true and fat victims, "holocausts full of marrow," which are offered by contrite and humble hearts, and which those who practice this control and fervor of spirit, of which we have spoken, with effectual power can sing: "Let my prayer be set forth in Thy sight as the incense: let the lifting up of my hands be an evening sacrifice" (Ps. 140:2).[71]

It is in the writings of Cassian that we find the first clear description of the practice of prayer designated by the Greeks as *monologistos*,[72] a form in which a single prayer formula is constantly repeated in order to help focus the mind and heart in order to sustain unceasing prayer. One such formula presented by Cassian is Psalm 69:2. In order to grow through the vicissitudes in prayer life and to deepen the interior disposition in prayer, Cassian advocated the need for a certain degree of spontaneity in prayer. Length in prayer usually meant an absence of spontaneity, so Cassian placed importance on the "short"

---

[68] *Inst.* 2:10. Also, "*Prayer in Early Western Monasticism*" by Adalbert de Vogüé, OSB, in WS 3, pp. 114ff.

[69] *Chapters on Prayer*, 151; Lk. 18:10 & Mt. 6:7.

[70] *Ibid.*, 98.

[71] *Conf.* 9:36.

[72] NJH, p. 242.

prayer formula and chose Psalm 69:2 as a formula that could be easily "repeated several hundred times a day by people who are preoccupied with other tasks."[73] According to Cassian,

> When you wake let it be the first thing to come into your mind, let it anticipate all your waking thoughts, let it when you rise from your bed send you down on your knees, and thence send you forth to all your work and business, and let it follow you about all day long. This you should think about, according to the Lawgiver's charge, "at home and walking forth on a journey" (Dt. 6:7), sleeping and waking. This you should write on the threshold and door of your mouth, this you should place on the walls of your house and in the recesses of your heart so that when you fall on your knees in prayer this may be your chant as you kneel, and when you rise up from it to go forth to all the necessary business of life it may be your constant prayer as you stand.[74]

Cassian recommended Ps. 69:2 as a method for continual prayer. There were many effects of using a single psalm verse. Hausherr states that

> the first effect of the psalm verse is to awaken every devout sentiment in our hearts; that is why Cassian called it a sacred formula (formula pietatis). Secondly, it helps to overcome and banish all temptations. Third, it is effective against every such spiritual infirmity as evil inclinations, evil feelings, vices especially of the flesh, illicit desires, bursts of anger, various dangers and occasions of sin. Fourth, it is powerful against dreams and illusions inspired by the devil. And finally, it is a means of retaining the continual memory of God and maintaining unceasing, assiduous prayer, without strain or difficulty.[75]

The Deus in adiutorium leads to the perfection of contemplation and to a greater degree of purity because, according to Cassian,[76]

> . . . it relies on no image of the imagination, nor on any speech or words, but it springs up like a spark from a burning coal in an ineffable surge of the heart and an inexhaustible alacrity of spirit. The

---

[73] Ibid., p. 206.
[74] Conf. 10:10.
[75] NJH, p. 203.
[76] Ibid., p. 204.

mind is carried beyond all material things that can be seen or felt and pours out its prayer with inutterable sighs and groanings.[77]

Other authors may have used psalm verses for prayer, but Cassian was probably the first to articulate this use of Scripture to develop continuous prayer, as centuries later would be witnessed to the use of the Jesus Prayer: Lord Jesus Christ, Son of God, have mercy on me a sinner.[78]

IS THERE PRAYER TO JESUS IN CASSIAN?

In the works of Cassian, if there is prayer to Jesus,[79] it is found in the symbiotic unity between growing in the example of Christ and spontaneous short prayer. It is in following the example of Christ that we acquire a certain internal disposition necessary for spiritual growth in prayer and it matures through spontaneous short prayer, often without audible words.[80] Hausherr mentions that "the person who prays tends spontaneously to use expressions that are most in accord with his own temperament"[81] and that the few ascetics who left some record of their prayer life all knew the importance of the interior disposition created by prayer. We are reminded by Hausherr that

> . . . in the gospels many people ask favors of the miracle-worker from Nazareth. Neither Matthew nor Mark nor John records any prayers containing the vocative, "Jesus." Mark 1:24 and 5:7 are not prayers but the cries of demons coming through the mouths of the possessed: "Jesus, son of the most high God, I implore you, do not torture me" (Mk. 5:7).[82]

While it may be true that the Jesus Prayer[83] is present in the four gospels in fragmentary form, we may be sure that the verse from Mk. 5:7 was

---

[77] *Conf.* 10:11.

[78] Cf. Luibheid, *John Cassian: Conferences, op. cit.*, p. 13. Conference 10:10 is an important stage in the origins of hesychasm and the Jesus Prayer.

[79] Cf. *Conf.* 15:3, 5, 7. Cassian mentions prayer to Jesus in the context of calling upon the name of Christ to help us transform our interior life through His Spirit.

[80] Mt. 11:28–29: ". . . learn from me, for I am gentle and humble in heart . . ."

[81] NJH, p. 205.

[82] *Ibid.*, pp. 194–195, 197.

[83] See footnote #78 above.

"not the model that inspired it, though there is a similarity in the initial words."[84]

Origen mentions supplication to Jesus and insists that the Christian make his prayer in and through Christ.[85] As Origen says,[86]

> . . . it is not foolish to offer supplication, intercession, and thanksgiving also to the saints. Moreover, two of them, I mean intercession and thanksgiving, may be addressed not only to the saints but also to other people, while supplication may be addressed only to the saints if someone is found to be a Paul or a Peter so as to help us by making us worthy of receiving the authority given them to forgive sins (cf. Mt. 9:6; Jn. 20:23) . . . If these kinds of prayer are to be offered to holy men, how much more must thanksgiving be addressed to Christ, who has benefited us so greatly by the will of the Father? Moreover, intercession must be addressed to Him, as Stephen says, "Lord, do not hold this sin against them" (Acts 7:60). Imitating the father of the lunatic we shall say, "I pray you, Lord, have mercy on my son"—or on me, or on any one at all (cf. Mt. 17:15; Lk. 9:38).

Gabriel Bunge admits the following in the case of Evagrius:

> Depending on the stage it (prayer) has attained, it is addressed to one of the three divine Persons, but also to Christ, the incarnate Logos. The prayers and requests for help and support in the suppression of temptations are mostly (although not exclusively) addressed to Christ, after the model of those who encountered him in his earthly existence.[87]

Evagrius suggests "praying to Christ in our nightly vigils" as well as addressing prayer to the Logos Himself.[88] He recommends "short and intense prayer" and reportedly gives us the instructions to unite our breath with the name of Jesus: "Join to every breath a sober invocation

---

[84] NJH, pp.194–195, 197.

[85] Cf. *Origen*, with trans. & intro. by Rowan A. Greer, The Classics of Western Spirituality Series, Paulist Press, New York, 1979, pp. 100–101.

[86] Origen, *On Prayer*, 14:6.

[87] "*The 'Spiritual Prayer': On the Trinitarian Mysticism of Evagrius of Pontus*," by Gabriel Bunge, MS 17 (1987), 198–199.

[88] *Praktikos*, 54; *Chapters on Prayer*, 50.

of the name of Jesus and the thought of death with humility. Both these practices bring great profit to the soul."[89]

While the invocation of Jesus was used to help develop an interiorly receptive disposition in prayer,[90] it was not in itself sufficient: "... even though when he is showing off he invokes the name of Christ, yet he is far from Christ, because in his pride of heart he does not follow his humble Teacher."[91] In *De Incarnatione*, Cassian implies a connection between the invocation of Jesus and freedom, an internal disposition allowing growth in purity of heart where the heart is at peace and bears the fruits of tranquillity and calmness. He states:

> ... again and again do we pray to Thee, O Lord Jesus, to whom we have ever prayed, that Thou wouldst give us words by opening our mouth "to the pulling down of strong-holds, destroying counsels, and every height that exalteth itself against the knowledge of God, and bringing into captivity every understanding unto Thine obedience": (2 Cor. 10:4–5) for he is indeed free, who has begun to be led captive by Thee.[92]

It is the growth in disposition toward unceasing prayer using the remembrance of Jesus through His invocation which allows for growth in purity of heart and internal peace. Cassian sees the example of Christ and His remembrance in short prayer as nurturing this growth.

PRAYER OF FIRE

In the ascending sequence of the journey in prayer there is intermingled by Cassian a peculiar form of prayer: fiery prayer—the *oratio ignita*. It is a sudden bursting forth in a wordless and ineffable elevation of the mind and heart to God. Monks in the earliest stages of prayer can even have some experience of it, for as Cassian in his practical optimism says, "in whatever degree any one stands, he is found sometimes to offer pure and devout prayers."[93]

---

[89] *Chapters on Prayer*, 98; cf. *Holy Fathers from the Philokalia*. Tr. by E. Kadloubovsky & G.E.H. Palmer, p. 113.

[90] "*The Invocation of the Divine Name in Sinaite Spirituality*" by Edward J. Ryan, ECQ 14, 4 (1961–1962), 245.

[91] *Conf.* 15:7.

[92] *De Incarn.* 7:1.

[93] *Conf.* 9:15.

Of the various degrees of contemplation mentioned by Cassian, the highest is the *oratio pura*,[94] a state of prayer also called *oratio iugis*.[95] Brief moments of this highest state of ineffable prayer that rises above human consciousness are referred to as *oratio ignita*; no words are uttered and the soul is so heavenly illuminated that it darts out to God:

> Sometimes however the mind which is advancing to that perfect state of purity and which is already beginning to be established in it, will take in all these at one and the same time, and like some incomprehensible and all-devouring flame, dart through them all and offer up to God inexpressible prayers of the purest force.[96]

The prayer of fire is spontaneous, sudden, and intense. "On the part of the monk, it's more passivity, waiting for the revelation of God than an active research of what radically overcomes his own strengths."[97] It is prayer which

> is brought about by the contemplation of God alone and by fervent love, by which the mind, transporting and flinging itself into love for Him, addresses God most familiarly as its own Father with a piety of its own[98] . . . ardent prayer which is known and tried by but very few, and which to speak more truly is ineffable; which transcends all human thoughts, and is distinguished . . . by no movement of the tongue, or utterance of words.[99]

Fiery prayer is God's gift. It is simply the normal fruition that bursts forth, by the grace of God, when vocal prayer is well made. Here

> . . . the mind enlightened by the infusion of that heavenly light describes in no human and confined language . . . expressing in the shortest possible space of time such great things that the mind when it returns to its usual condition cannot easily utter or relate . . . this

---

[94] *Ibid.*, 9.

[95] *Ibid.*, 10:8–10; 7:6.

[96] *Ibid.*, 9:15; see also *Conf.* 9:26. Cassian sees the spark-like prayer of contemplation as sometimes granted not just to those who have attained great purity of heart, but on occasion to those progressing along the way of virtue as well. It is in essence a God-granted mystical experience.

[97] Guy, *Jean Cassien: Vie et doctrine spirituelle, op. cit.*, p. 55.

[98] *Conf.* 9:18.

[99] *Ibid.*, 9:25.

condition our Lord also similarly prefigured by the form of those supplications which, when he retired alone in the mountain He is said to have poured forth in silence.[100]

Cassian himself received this gift:

> . . . by the kind gift of the Lord I remember that I was often caught up into such an ecstasy as to forget that I was clothed with the burden of a weak body, and my soul on a sudden forgot all external notions and entirely cut itself off from all material objects, so that neither my eyes nor ears performed their proper functions.[101]

Just as the prayer of fire is spontaneous and a gift of God, so too is the concomitant gift of tears, whose plentiful supply, Cassian assures us, is not in our own power.[102] In fact, the prayer of fire may be impossible without the tears which help us purify our affections. As Cassian says: " . . . sometimes the mind . . . is filled with such overwhelming conviction and grief that it cannot express it except by floods of tears."[103] Tears release the news of the inner struggle we are all involved in, but try earnestly to hide. The term referred to actual weeping, but it was also a euphemism for an organic transformation of the person: a transformation which had a direct influence on personal prayer.

Cassian does make mention of "the gift of tears as an attendant circumstance,"[104] and relates the importance of this gift in quoting Isaac:[105]

> . . . not every kind of shedding of tears is produced by one feeling or one virtue. For in one way does that weeping originate which is caused by the pricks of our sins smiting our heart, of which we read: "I have laboured in my groanings, every night I will wash my bed; I will water my couch with my tears."[106] . . . In another, that which arises from the contemplation of eternal good things and the desire of

---

[100] *Ibid.*

[101] *Ibid.*, 19:4.

[102] *Ibid.*, 9:28.

[103] *Ibid.*, 9:27.

[104] *Spiritual Terminology in the Latin Translations of the Vita Antonii* by L.Th.A. Lorié, Nijmegen, 1955, p. 159; see *Conf.* 9:27–30.

[105] *Conf.* 9:29.

[106] Ps. 6:7.

that future glory, owing to which even richer wellsprings of tears
burst forth from uncontrollable delights and boundless exultation,
while our soul is athirst for the mighty Living God, saying, "When
shall I come and appear before the presence of God? My tears have
been my meat day and night."[107] . . . In another way do the tears flow
forth, which without any conscience of deadly sin, yet still proceed
from the fear of hell and the recollection of that terrible judgment,
with the terror of which the prophet was smitten and prayed to God,
saying: "Enter not into judgment with Thy servant, for in Thy sight
shall no man living be justified."[108] . . . There is too another kind of
tears, which are caused not by knowledge of one's self but by the
hardness and sins of others; whereby Samuel is described as having
wept for Saul, and both the Lord in the gospel and Jeremiah in former
days for the city of Jerusalem.[109]

Tears were of marked importance because they were always exterior
signs of the interior struggle between the passions and the spirit's desire
for God. They were physical manifestations of a very profound
ontological transformation occurring within man's life; he is becoming
God by participation. The cause of these tears arises from God's gift to
man to see his sinfulness and separateness and the experience of the
abundant mercy and love of God. In humility we seek God, and He
graces us with the perfection of that humility.

Nevertheless, as Hausherr admits,[110] Cassian "has a low opinion of
'forced tears,'[111] a point on which he differs from some of his Eastern
brethren, notably the one he follows faithfully in many other matters,
Evagrius Ponticus." While Evagrius, in his treatise on prayer, tells
monks "pray first for the gift of tears so that by means of sorrow you
may soften your native rudeness,"[112] Cassian believes that

from these tears those are vastly different which are squeezed out
from dry eyes while the heart is hard: and although we cannot believe
that these are altogether fruitless (for the attempt to shed them is made

[107] *Ibid.*, 42:3–4.

[108] *Ibid.*, 142:2.

[109] Cf. Jer. 9:1; Ps. 101:10; Mt. 5:3.

[110] *Penthos: The Doctrine of Compunction in the Christian East* by Irénée Hausherr,
S.J., CSS 53 (1982), 83.

[111] *Conf.* 9:30.

[112] *Chapters on Prayer*, 5.

with a good intention, especially by those who have not yet been able to attain to perfect knowledge or to be thoroughly cleansed from the stains of past or present sins), yet certainly the flow of tears ought not to be thus forced out by those who have already advanced to the love of virtue, nor should the weeping of the outward man be with great labour attempted, as even if it is produced it will never attain the rich copiousness of spontaneous tears. For it will rather cast down the soul of the suppliant by his endeavours, and humiliate him, and plunge him in human affairs and draw him away from the celestial heights, wherein the awed mind of one who prays should be steadfastly fixed, and will force it to relax its hold on its prayers and grow sick from barren and forced tears.[113]

---

[113] *Conf.* 9:30.

CHAPTER 2

DISPOSITIONS FOR GOOD PRAYER

The computerization of society inundated with the drive toward immediate gratification highlights the need for some form of patience. Although we appreciate the psychological need of patience in raising children, we nevertheless find it difficult to transfer this appreciation to the spiritual realm, especially in nurturing a God-centered internal disposition for prayer. The works of Cassian highlight the importance of this need, especially in the journey of spiritual perfection through prayer. There is a dynamic growth process in prayer for Cassian and it is conditioned "little by little" from the state of the soul before prayer to its condition during prayer.[1]

1. *PATIENCE*

Cassian is very clear that whatever level of virtue a monk exercises, whatever holiness he cultivates, all of it ultimately comes from and is made possible by God. One becomes spiritual through the participation of the Holy Spirit. Among the many fruits of the Holy Spirit is patience, and its absence hampers the efficacy of prayer.[2] Thus if we can speak of a kind of religious heroism in terms of the monk's search and struggle for perfection by means of prayer, it is always the case that religious heroism for Cassian is a charism given by God; to attain perfection is, as St. Paul says, to "fight the great fight" and to gain the crown.[3]

---

[1] *Conf.*, 10:8. See also 9:3,16.

[2] *Inst.* 9:11; see Gal. 5:22–23.

[3] *Conf.* 1:5. See also *Inst.* 5:17.

Cassian's language for the most part is that of intense combat, never-ending struggle,[4] and the possibility of victory for the perseverant. Although the journey of the soul in prayer described by him is just as much a defensive battle against the encroachments by evil and demonic forces as it is a progressive development of the virtues, growth in one's prayer life for Cassian is intimately connected with a strong edifice of all the virtues.[5] It is the preparation before prayer that is important for him in the defensive and progressive development[6] of virtues so that the soul can be prepared through discernment to act when the time comes and through action gradually to grow in perfection and as a consequence conform more to the image of God.

For Antony, to grow in perfection meant to gain control of our passions.[7] Perfection for Cassian is dynamic and full of movement toward the love of God. For the person who seeks genuine perfection, there awaits those things which used to seem beyond the powers of men.[8] The life of perfection makes such things not only possible but also truly rewarding. As O. Chadwick says, "the entire direction of Cassian's thought was toward the private, 'mystical' experience of the divine."[9] Only within the environment, provided in an ascetical tradition, can the contemplative life of prayer thrive. This ascetical tradition helps to place all spiritual gifts in perspective. The power to perform exorcisms or healings is a gift from God, but it is just one of the many charisms which God offers to men who seek him through prayer. More impressive than any ability to heal or even to raise the dead are the gifts of humility and of patience,[10] especially with respect to growth in prayer. As Cassian says,

> We pray when we promise that despising secular honors and scorning earthly riches we will cleave to the Lord in all sorrow of heart and

---

[4] The dynamic of inner "struggle" (or *pali* in Greek) is important for Cassian during the journey in prayer. It is "the struggle against" (or *i pali pros* in Greek) the powers of evil during the journey in prayer which Cassian highlights (see Eph. 6:12 in *Inst.* 5:18, 19 and *Conf.* 7:21, 33, 8:2, 13:14).

[5] *Conf.* 9:2.

[6] *Ibid.*, 10:14.

[7] *Vita Antonii*, 55.

[8] *Conf.*, pref.: 1; see Luibheid, *op. cit.*, p. 10.

[9] Luibheid, *op. cit.*, p. 30.

[10] Chadwick, *op. cit.*, pp. 95–96, 100.

humility of spirit. We pray when we promise that we will ever
maintain the most perfect purity of body and steadfast patience, or
when we vow that we will utterly root out of our heart the roots of
anger or of sorrow that worketh death.[11]

Cassian was a follower of Evagrius in his development of basic
prayer life[12] and Evagrius appreciated the fact that "the contemplative's
humility consist above all in not forgetting to ascribe the entire merit of
victories over his enemies to the grace of God."[13] Evagrius was aware
of the importance of growth in humility, especially for progress in the
spiritual journey in prayer: "strive to cultivate a deep humility and the
malice of the demons shall not touch your soul."[14] Nevertheless, at the
time of temptation, Evagrius especially appreciated patience: "the time
of temptation is not the time to leave one's cell, devising plausible
pretexts. Rather, stand there firmly and be patient."[15] Indeed, Evagrius
knew that patience was a significant factor for growth during prayer:
"whatever difficulty you patiently endure through love of wisdom will
reap ripe fruits at the time of prayer,"[16] and "if you know how to
practice patience you shall ever pray with joy."[17] According to Cassian,
patience was to be looked for ". . . as the consequence of your own
humility and longsuffering which does depend on your own will."[18]
Peace of heart, for Cassian, resided in one's own control[19] and "patience
had to be maintained, not in words, but in inward tranquillity of heart."[20]
The perfection of patience was important in Cassian's view for growth
in peace of heart:

> We need not then seek for our peace in externals, nor fancy that
> another person's patience can be of any use to the faults of our

---

[11] *Conf.* 9:12. See also 15:7.

[12] *Les "Képhalaia gnostica" d'Évagre le Pontique* by Antoine Guillaumont, ed. du
Deuil, Paris, 1962, p. 77.

[13] SHI, p. 89.

[14] *Chapters on Prayer*, 96.

[15] *Praktikos*, 28.

[16] *Chapters on Prayer*, 19.

[17] *Ibid.*, 23.

[18] *Inst.* 4:42.

[19] *Ibid.*, 8:17.

[20] *Conf.* 16:22.

impatience. For just as "the kingdom of God is within you,"[21] so "a man's foes are they of his own household."[22] For no one is more my enemy than my own heart which is truly the one of my household closest to me . . . For where those of our own household are not opposed to us, there also the kingdom of God is secured in peace of heart . . . if I am injured, the fault is not owing to the other's attack, but to my own impatience.[23]

Cassian realized the importance of growing in "a lasting and unbroken patience" because

What greater injury can happen to the soul than for it, owing to some sudden blindness from rage, to lose the brightness of the true and eternal light and to fail of the sight of Him "Who is meek and lowly of heart?" (Mt.11:29)[24]

One enemy of growth in peace of heart is uncontrollable or "spiritually unprofitable"[25] anger. Antony urged his followers to listen to the words of St. Paul: ". . . never let the sun set on your anger or else you will give the devil a foothold."[26] While it is Evagrius who points out that anger disturbs the normal activity of the mind[27] and that "turbid anger is calmed by the singing of psalms, by patience, and by almsgiving,"[28] it is Cassian who understood anger as destructive to growth in purity of prayer[29] and saw patience as helping to diffuse this passion:

---

[21] Cf. Lk. 17:21.

[22] Cf. Mt. 10:36.

[23] *Conf.* 18:16.

[24] *Ibid.*, 19:14.

[25] "Spiritually unprofitable" in the sense that "God's righteousness is never served by man's anger" (James 1:20; cf. *Inst.* 8:1). Even Cassian admits that there are cases in which anger is useful and profitable (cf. *Inst.* 8:7). The role of anger is to fight against the demons, not to use it against our neighbor, as expressed by Climacus in his *Scalae*, 26.

[26] *Vita Antonii*, 55. See Eph. 4:26–27; Cassian utilizes this passage in the following four places in his works: *Inst.* 8:9; *Conf.* 2:4, 16:6, 17.

[27] *Praktikos*, 63.

[28] *Ibid.*, 15.

[29] *Conf.* 9:3. A recent description of anger as a "barrier to prayer" for Cassian is given by Kenneth C. Russell in *Healing the Heart: Desert Wisdom for a Busy World*, Novalis, 1993, pp. 56–57.

And in truth it is a greater miracle to root out from one's own flesh the incentives to wantonness than to cast out unclean spirits from the bodies of others, and it is a grander sign to restrain the fierce passions of anger by the virtue of patience than to command the powers of the air.[30]

Cassian understood that growth in humility and patience was the concomitant effect of growth in prayer to provide for the inward tranquillity of heart. He saw patience as key to this growth:

We ought then to restrain every movement of anger and moderate it under the direction of discretion, . . . a fool is inflamed by the passion of his anger to avenge himself; but a wise man, by the ripeness of his counsel and moderation *little by little diminishes* it, and gets rid of it . . . so your mind will be enlarged with wide long-suffering and patience, and will have within it safe recesses of counsel, in which the foul smoke of anger will be received and be diffused and forthwith vanish away.[31]

The practice by way of prayer of any of the virtues discussed in the *Conferences* is for Cassian in a real sense a charismatic reality because all holy things have God as their author.

As wonderful as physical cures may be, they nevertheless mostly pertain to the "exterior man" and do not always touch the "inner man," the inner life, the life of prayer; such gifts usually remain inferior in quality to the ultimate gifts and virtues that advance and incarnate the monastic life of prayer. Cassian utilizes the lives of holy men as examples of this advancement and incarnation because they are extraordinary for the inner life they witness to in following Christ. For Cassian, growth in the virtues, especially humility and patience, nurtures growth in faith-filled confidence during prayer, where one no longer depends on externals but now relies on a God-centered internal disposition, the "inner man."[32] It is the profundity and strength of the inner man which distinguishes the monk, especially his life of prayer. Cassian places emphasis on the fact that Christ looks not only at external actions but also at the internal disposition created by means of prayer, the internal movements and purity of the inner soul in which ideally "the inner man

---

[30] *Conf.* 15:8.

[31] *Ibid.*, 16:27. Emphasis mine.

[32] *Ibid.*, 18:16.

may not even silently be disturbed in itself at the blows of the outward man."[33]

2. *STRUGGLE AGAINST SIN: TEMPTATION*

One of the growing trends in our television/computer-oriented society is the need to be responsible consumers, materially as well as spiritually. Television networks find it monetarily convenient to boost ratings by preying on basic human instincts, probing regions deemed off-limits, and exploring taboo subjects under the guise of satisfying customer interests; computer accessibility (especially now through the Internet) aids in testing the limits and embracing rapid leaps from one broken taboo to the next. Often the desire for immediate gratification obscures any feeling of responsibility and there develops an inability to establish limits of behavior and controls. This desire of immediacy in a culture of excess often results in a velocity of lifestyle that makes it convenient not to think about behavior and its consequences, not to mention a sense of evil.

While there is a desire to minimize the likelihood of being deceived and a need to reduce general vulnerability to temptation, the problem of evil continues to vex even the responsible consumer in the spiritual journey, where it is often neglected, especially in prayer. The works of Cassian are relevant to these concerns, especially the need (1) to deal with the inner struggle through growth in discretion, and (2) to patiently persevere in prayer during times of temptation, for in the absence of the recollection of God, temptation cannot be far behind.[34]

INNER STRUGGLE

In the words of A. de Vogüé, the notion of monastic life for Cassian is "entirely dynamic, indeed warlike. It is about an interminable progress, a fight without end against sin . . . a constant struggle."[35] According to Tomáš Špidlík,[36]

---

[33] *Ibid.*, 16:22.

[34] *Ibid.*, 7:24 and 8:19.

[35] "Monachisme et Église dans la pensée de Cassien" by Adalbert de Vogüé, O.S.B., *Théologie de la vie monastique* (Études sur la Tradition patristique), Aubier, 1961, p. 232.

[36] Špidlík, *op. cit.*, p. 235.

The desert is the demons' very favorite domain, and the monk who withdraws there will confront them in face-to-face combat.[37] The demonology expressed in the *Life of Antony*,[38] in the work of Evagrius[39] and Cassian[40] became classical of the desert.

The desert with its starkness and simplicity is not a place of superficial experiences. The depth of one's identity is often tested and experienced in the desert. Nevertheless, few of us can go to the physical desert to find God. Our desert is normally created within ourselves; a desert in which one's ears grow attuned to the inner silence[41] of one's heart—a silence best realized in the desert's solitude.[42] Solitude is the furnace in which one's transformation into the image of God[43] takes place. It is all alone in the solitude of one's heart that temptation happens—temptation which is a unique and very lonely thing and permeates the journey in prayer.

Jesus Himself experienced the reality of temptation.[44] As Scripture reminds us, the enemy will be back.[45] "They simply attack again in another way,"[46] as Antony admits, but "we need not fear their suggestions, for by prayer and fasting and by faith in the Lord they are brought down immediately."[47] Faith in the Lord is for Antony the desire to allow the Word of God and His will to shape each moment of our lives through His Spirit. Prayer for Antony is seen as a life of conflict in which evil forces are encountered and defeated, for "as Scripture says,

---

[37] Bamberger, *op. cit.*, p. 16; *Praktikos*, 5.

[38] Cf. Louis Bouyer, *La vie de saint Antoine*, Abbaye de Wandrille, 1950, 103ff.

[39] *Évagre le Pontique: Traité Pratique ou Le Moine* by A. and C. Guillaumont, Tome 1, SC 170, 94ff.

[40] *"Cassien"* by Michel Olphe-Galliard, S.J., DSAM 2: 242.

[41] For an appreciation of growth in unceasing prayer as the concomitant result of the deepening of the inner silence of one's heart, see Chapter 2 (part 2 above) or my paper entitled *"Incessant Prayer and John Cassian"* in Dk. 28, 2 (1995) 74–80. Also, see *Silence* by Ambrose G. Wathen, O.S.B., CSS 22, 1973.

[42] Cf. *Conf.* 7:26, 14:4, 19:10, 24:18.

[43] See footnote #26 in Chapter 1.

[44] Mt. 4:1–13.

[45] Lk. 4:13.

[46] *Athanasius, The Life of Antony & the Letter to Marcellinus* by R.C. Gregg, translation & introduction, New York, 1980, #23, p. 48.

[47] *Ibid.*; also, *Vita Antonii*, 4, 5, 27, 30, 40, 47.

let us keep our heart in all watchfulness.[48] For *we have terrible and villainous enemies*—the evil demons, and *our contending is against these*."[49] During his thirty-five years in the desert, Antony was tempted in many different ways.[50]

Temptation, Origen insists, is always an identity experience revealing who we are and who we are meant to become.[51] The inner struggle (temptation) or "wrestling against"[52] evil is likened to warfare or an athletic contest. Origen uses the scriptural account of Eve's easy deception from Gen 3:1–6 to highlight the use of temptation,[53] and reminds us

> that the person who is *about to come to prayer* should withdraw for a little and prepare himself, and so become more attentive and active for the whole of his prayer. He should *cast away all temptation* and troubling thoughts and remind himself so far as he is able of the Majesty whom he approaches.[54]

Evagrius follows Origen in using the warfare and wrestling imagery with respect to the inner struggle against temptation.[55] For Evagrius, "wisdom is not won except by a battle"[56] and he views sin[57] as a possibility because human beings are vulnerable to deception:

---

[48] Prov. 4:23.

[49] Gregg, *op. cit.*, p. 47. Emphasis mine; Also, *Vita Antonii*, 21.

[50] "*On 'Discernment of Spirits' in the Early Church*" by Joseph T. Lienhard, S.J., TS, 1980, p. 516.

[51] *Origen* by Rowan A. Greer, *op. cit.*, p. 161.

[52] *On Prayer*, 33:1. See Greer, *op. cit.*, p. 162. "The struggle against" (*i pali pros* in Greek) temptation attracted the ascetics, who were often called the "strugglers" (*agonistai* in Greek). The dynamic of inner "wrestling" or "struggle" (cf. Eph 6:12) is important for Cassian during the journey in prayer. He highlights the fact that we "wrestle against" (*colluctatio adversus* in Latin; cf. *Inst.* 5:18, 19; *Conf.* 7:21, 33, 8:2, 13:14) demons in this inner journey.

[53] *Ibid.*, p. 161; Origen, *On Prayer*, 29:18.

[54] *Ibid.*, p. 164. Emphasis mine. See Origen, *On Prayer*, 31:2.

[55] Evagrius, *Praktikos*, 72.

[56] *Ibid.*, 73.

[57] The distinction between sin and temptation rests with the consent to the evil thought (and not with its mere presence) as Evagrius states in *Praktikos* 74–75: "Temptation is the lot of the monk, for thoughts which darken his mind will inevitably arise from the part of his soul that is the seat of passion. The sin that a monk has particularly to watch out for is that of giving mental consent to some forbidden pleasure."

When you are praying against some evil thoughts and you find that you are freed from them readily, examine how this comes about lest you fall into some hidden trap, and by being *deceived* betray yourself.[58]

One example of a subtle form of deception for Evagrius was the "holy angel" imagery:

It is proper that you be advised about another ruse. The demons divide up into two groups for a time, and when they see you calling out for help against the one group and others make their appearance under the form of angels who drive away the first group. They have in mind *to deceive you into believing that they are holy angels in all truth.*[59]

J. Driscoll rightly points out that this passage "speaks of demons appearing as angels and trying to convince the one to whom they appear into thinking that they are holy angels,"[60] and yet they are, as Evagrius says, "the teachings of heretics: *angels of death*. The one who receives them looses his soul."[61] In many of the cases related by Cassian there exist stories concerning deceived holy men of the desert.[62] In many of these stories the devil takes on the appearance of an *angel of light*[63] while manifesting the ultimate in deceit, especially in the inner struggle during the journey in prayer.[64]

Evagrius' view of temptation in the inner struggle was heavily influenced through a life of conflict with demons: a life vulnerable to demonic attacks for not having kept watch over *praktike*, which basically consists in the art of learning to combat evil thoughts.[65] As J. E. Bamberger points out, "of the hundred chapters that make up the

---

[58] Evagrius, *Prayer*, 133. Emphasis mine. See also, *Prayer*, 134, 94, 95.

[59] *Ibid.*, 95. Emphasis mine.

[60] *The "Ad Monachos" of Evagrius Ponticus, its structure and a select commentary*, by Jeremy Driscoll, O.S.B., SA 104, Rome, 1991, footnote 183, p. 149.

[61] Evagrius, *"Ad Monachos"* 125. Emphasis mine. See H. Gressmann (ed.), *Nonnenspiegel und Mönchsspiegel des Euagrios Pontikos*, TU 39, 4 (1913) 143–165.

[62] Cf. *Conf.* 2:5, 7, 8.

[63] *Discretio*, by Fr. Dingjan, O.S.B., Assen, Van Gorcum & Co., 1967, p. 250.

[64] Cf. *Conf.* 10:10, 9:34, 9:6, 10:11.

[65] Guillaumont, *op. cit.*, 38–112.

Praktikos, demons are mentioned in sixty-seven."[66] Evagrius understood that

> to be troubled by a thought is to be troubled by a demon. The true battle of the monk is with the demons themselves. Thoughts are the means used by the demons to trouble the monk . . . The demons have as their goal keeping the monk from reaching passionlessness . . . *Demons* inspire *thoughts*, and these, when they are allowed to linger, unleash the *passions* in us.[67]

Demons represented a key source of temptation for Evagrius and were a direct influence on the monk's spiritual life, especially his prayer life. If not initially successful in their inducements, as Evagrius explains, "the demons withdraw a bit and observe to see which of the virtues he neglects in the meantime. Then all of a sudden they attack him from this point and ravage the poor fellow."[68] For the holy ones of God there is no rest from the presence of evil, especially for growth in purity of heart by means of prayer.

Evil confuses since it is both repelling and alluring. Vices often seen as repellent become virtues needed for survival. Of the eight vices, which he classified in detail,[69] Evagrius appreciated the importance of greed,[70] since it played such a central role in the temptations of Christ.[71] Cassian developed this appreciation in realizing that "in order to quell anger," which he understood as destructive to growth in purity of prayer,[72] "avarice must be trampled under foot"[73] for "it will grow by feeding on itself."[74]

---

[66] Bamberger, *op. cit.*, p. 4.

[67] J. Driscoll, *op. cit.*, pp. 13–14.

[68] Evagrius, *Praktikos*, 44.

[69] *Ibid.*, 6. Cassian develops these eight vices (gluttony, fornication, avarice, anger, melancholy, *acedia*, vainglory, pride) for the West in his *Inst.* 5–12; see Chadwick, *op. cit.*, pp. 94–95 and SHI, pp. 248–256.

[70] For Cassian, avarice (in Greek *philargyria*, the love of money) "is a root of all kinds of evil" (1 Tim. 6:10) [*Inst.* 7:6] for it's "the worship of idols" (Col. 3:5) [*Inst.* 7:7].

[71] See footnote #44 above.

[72] *Conf.* 9:3.

[73] *Ibid.*, 5:10.

[74] *Inst.* 7:21.

GROWTH IN DISCRETION

Covetousness presents a challenge to any society immersed in materialism which exploits the theory that there are certain things that people will not give up, regardless of how poor they are. In a culture of excess, moderation becomes important through growth in discretion.[75] As prayer matures, discretion helps to moderate excesses, where moderation is not the *discretio* itself but only its first fruit.[76] For Cassian, it is clear that

> We ought then with all our might to strive for the virtue of discretion by the power of humility, as it will keep us uninjured by either extreme . . . we pass on with due moderation, and walk between the two extremes, under the guidance of discretion.[77]

Cassian understands discretion as strengthening prayer, for "it is clearly shown that no virtue can possibly be perfectly acquired or continue without the grace of discretion."[78]

All aspects of discretion for Cassian presupposed as a foundation the discernment of good and evil spirits, especially for growth in prayer. Even manual labor had to be seen within proper limits of discerned control so that it remained an aid and not a hindrance to prayer.[79] For Cassian, it was important to control the passions before trying to destroy them.[80] It's certainly in dealing with temptations and mastering the passions that he understood would provide a disposition for good prayer. Cassian is concerned with the task of gradually undoing our ego-centered personalities. He understands the importance of destroying our attachment to the ordinary world while trying not to be consumed by the future. Reflective meditation from Scripture is used to aid constant recollection of the Lord.[81] One way that he used to help gain control

---

[75] For Cassian, discretion is the charism of proper judgment which helps one avoid the sin of excess in any undertaking and teaches one always to walk along the "royal road" (cf. *Conf.* 2:2, 10:11).

[76] Dingjan, *op. cit.*, p. 74.

[77] *Conf.* 2:16.

[78] *Ibid.*, 2:4.

[79] Cf. *Inst.* 2:14, 3:2, 2:12; also, *Conf.* 9:5–6.

[80] *Conf.* 14:3.

[81] *Ibid.*, 1:22.

over passions was the repetition of a Scriptural verse.[82] In fact, Cassian follows Evagrius in calling for unceasing prayer,[83] for it is growth in disposition toward unceasing prayer using the remembrance of Jesus through His invocation which allows for growth in purity of heart and interior peace.[84] For Cassian, "according to the measure of its purity . . . each mind is both raised and moulded in its prayer."[85]

PERSEVERANCE IN PRAYER

There exists a direct relationship for Cassian between perseverance in prayer and the ability to deal with temptation, whether a troubled subconscious or a demon. While his demonology is influenced by Evagrius,[86] Cassian follows Evagrius, who warns that "perfect purity of heart develops in the soul after the victory over all the demons whose function it is to offer opposition to the ascetic life."[87] As A. & C. Guillaumont make clear, "the demons cannot touch the soul, but only the body that they weaken to the point of obscuring the intelligence."[88] The monks encounter the demons in all of their power and wiles, and such encounters are significant moments in the journey to God in prayer. Indeed an important factor behind the great reverence for these monks is the virtue of perseverance shown in tangling with the evil ones, sometimes in literal face-to-face combat.

Cassian's language for the most part is that of intense combat, never-ending struggle,[89] and the possibility of victory for the perseverant. The demons are a most potent and dangerous force to be battled each and every day. Interestingly enough there is the claim that the demons possess a body, though it is a very fine one—like the air

---

[82] *Ibid.*, 10:10.

[83] See Chapter 1 (part 2 above). Even Evagrius admitted that "he who prays unceasingly escapes temptations" (cf. *Ad Monachos* 37).

[84] *Ibid.*, p. 86.

[85] *Conf.* 16:22.

[86] *"Demon dans la plus ancienne litterature monastique"* by Antoine et Claire Guillaumont, DSAM 3 (1957), 189–212.

[87] Evagrius, *Praktikos*, 60. See also 77.

[88] *"Relations sur la vie des moines"* by A. & C. Guillaumont, DSAM 3 (1954), 208–209.

[89] See footnote #52 above.

itself.[90] By viewing each monk, the demons are able to tell whether their inducements have taken the desired root. Cassian makes clear that

> . . . unclean spirits cannot make their way into those whose bodies they are going to seize upon, in any other way than by first taking possession of their minds and thoughts. And *when they have robbed them of fear and the recollection of God and spiritual meditation, they boldly advance upon them.*[91]

Cassian utilizes the example of Christ to illustrate the importance of the persistent recollection of God and spiritual meditation, for

> . . . no man, except our Lord and Saviour, can keep his naturally wandering mind always fixed on the contemplation of God so as never to be carried away from it through the love of something in this world.[92]

Through a discussion of Christ's temptations and victory, Cassian emphasizes "the differences between the sanctity of the monk and the immaculate life of Christ."[93] It is growth in sanctity of life through perseverance in prayer which Cassian sees as helping to overcome and prevent temptations. The power of Christ received by means of prayer helps in the prevention, but still it is a defensive battle in the journey to God, as Evagrius readily admitted[94] and Cassian emphasizes:

> . . . the blessed Anthony proved and established . . . that demons cannot possibly find an entrance into the mind or body of anyone, nor have they the power of overwhelming the soul of anyone, unless they

---

[90] Cf. *Conf.* 7:13. According to Cassian, the origin of the demons lies in the fall of heavenly angels who had been created before visible creation (*Conf.* 8:7–8). Just as the heavenly angels vary according to their rank and power, so too do the demons vary in their fallen state. Though they carry with them great power, this power does have limits. Cassian relates a story from Serenus, who tells his questioner Germanus that demons cannot know the "heart" of the person (*Conf.* 7:13). Demonic knowledge of a person's state of soul is possible only through a demon's observance of one's conduct and public character. And thus their power to know the inner life is no different from that of humans.

[91] *Conf.* 7:24. Emphasis mine. See also, 7:12, 15.

[92] *Ibid.*, 23:8.

[93] Chadwick, *op. cit.*, pp. 108–109. See *Conf.* 22:9–12; 5:5–6; 24:17.

[94] *Praktikos*, 42.

have first deprived it of all holy thoughts, and made it empty and free from spiritual meditation.[95]

For Cassian, the heroism of those on the road to sanctity in overcoming temptation is essentially tied to an understanding of the inner life, the life of the virtues and perseverance in prayer.

It is the gradual spiritual growth of the inner life by way of perseverance in prayer which brings about a more heated combat with the demons and temptations. In his authoritative study, Chadwick argues that Cassian's

> treatment of the fight with demons is ethically more subtle than the treatment in the *Life of Antony*. The demons of Cassian are indeed of the Greek tradition. They fill the air, have bodies invisible like air, are subject to chieftains, fight among themselves, provoke nations to war, and are angels fallen from heaven.[96]

But what has this to do with the hermits, the holy ones of God, who live, work, and pray in the desert? As Evagrius admits,[97] it is these powers of darkness against which the monks must work and fight. Indeed, "hard work" ("great application and endurance"; *kopos* in Greek)[98] and "perseverance"[99] ("patient endurance"; *hypomone* in Greek) are needed in the spiritual life—nothing is automatic. Even education alone is not sufficient, as Evagrius implies when he asks Arsenius "how is it that we, with all our education and our wide knowledge get no-where, while these Egyptian peasants acquire so many virtues?" And Arsenius

---

[95] *Conf.* 8:19.

[96] Chadwick, *op. cit.*, pp. 96–97.

[97] *Praktikos*, 5.

[98] Hausherr, *Penthos*, *op. cit.*, p. 76.

[99] Evagrius, *Prayer*, 19, 34, 88; *Praktikos*, 89. Also, see Driscoll, *op. cit.*, p. 55: "If the spirit of listlessness mounts you, do not leave your house; and do not turn aside in that hour from profitable wrestling. For like someone making money shine, so will your heart be made to glow" (*Ad Monachos* 55). According to Driscoll (p. 224), "the monk must stay and fight. *Ad Monachos* 55 calls the fight a profitable wrestling. The wrestling is profitable because though this demon 'moves all his legions to make the monk quit his cell and flee the stadium,' when the struggle is over, 'a peaceful state and an ineffable joy follow in the soul' (*Praktikos* 12). This is because one of the most difficult of all the demons has been defeated, and now the monk is on the verge of passionlessness." For a relationship between "spiritually unprofitable" wrestling and growth in prayer, see the first section in this chapter.

answers him: "We indeed get nothing from our secular education, but these Egyptian peasants acquire the virtues by hard work."[100] Cassian understands the need for hard work and perseverance, especially during the journey in prayer, for "no virtue is acquired without effort,"[101] and "the aim of every monk and the perfection of his heart tends to continual and unbroken *perseverance in prayer*."[102]

3. *SELF-CONTROL*

Because of his concern for the "inner man," Cassian places importance on the heart, which he describes as the sanctuary of the Word of God, and gives prime emphasis to what he calls a principal virtue of purity of heart.[103] He sees purity of heart as the immediate aim or goal of the spiritual life,[104] and it is gradually achieved through prayer and the disappearance of a modified form of the eight vices of which Evagrius spoke. For Cassian, it is important to control the passions before trying to destroy them; it is control guided by discretion.[105]

Growth in prayer is the concomitant result of the gradual replacing of our sinful desires by a new and better energy from God. For Cassian, it is movement toward the ideal of Evagrian *apatheia*,[106] or dispassion, freedom from passion. It is a state of reintegration and spiritual freedom, not the absence of all feeling. This state of reintegration and self-control is an integral part of a growing state of prayer, for as Cassian says, "if a man is not able to control passions, which are openly manifest and are but small, how will he be able with temperate discretion to fight against

---

[100] *The Sayings of the Desert Fathers. The Alphabetical Collection.* Translated, with a foreword by Benedicta Ward, SLG, and Preface by Metropolitan Anthony of Sourozh; Cistercian Publications Inc., Kalamazoo, Michigan, 1984, Arsenius #5, p. 10.

[101] *Conf.* 7:6.

[102] *Ibid.*, 9:2. Emphasis mine.

[103] *Inst.* 8:20; *Conf.* 1:5, 7, 14:9–10.

[104] *Conf.* 1:4.

[105] *Ibid.*, 5:10, 14:3, 16:27.

[106] On the whole, Evagrius understood *apatheia* not negatively but positively. It is not apathy in the modern sense of the word but the replacing of our sinful desires by a new and better energy from God. It refers to a state of the soul, a phase in the process of growth in prayer toward perfection; see *Praktikos*, 64, and note the concept of *hesychasm*.

those which are secret, and excite him when none are there to see?"[107] Even the peace of our mind lies in our own control:

> The chief part then of our improvement and peace of mind must not be made to depend on another's will, which cannot possibly be subject to our authority, but it lies rather in *our own control*. And so the fact that we are not angry ought not to result from another's perfection, but from our own virtue, which is acquired, not by somebody else's patience, but by our own long-suffering.[108]

Cassian follows Evagrius' doctrine of *apatheia*, but he retains that sense of reality which in this point is also characteristic of Origen.[109] He is only too well aware how relative is all perfection in this life on earth.[110] Transmitting Evagrius's teaching to the West, Cassian, although never using the term itself, renders *apatheia* as *puritas cordis*,[111] a "purity of heart," which allows one to see, feel, or taste the will of God. It is the positive conception of charity, as found in 1 Cor. 13:3, which Cassian equates with purity of heart.

Progress in the spiritual life for Cassian was directly linked to growth in prayer, since "the aim of every monk and the perfection of his heart tends to continual and unbroken perseverance in prayer."[112] Cassian appreciates the importance of a repetitive focus on a prayer as well as neither fighting nor focusing on intruding thoughts.[113] Even manual labor has to be seen within proper limits of discerned control so that it remains an aid and not a hindrance to prayer.[114] To grow in perfection means to grow in the virtues, especially humility and patience, and to gain control of the thoughts, feelings, and passions.

---

[107] *Inst.* 5:20.

[108] *Ibid.*, 8:17. Emphasis mine.

[109] Lorie, *op. cit.*, pp. 123–124.

[110] *Ibid.*, p. 124. See Chadwick, *op. cit.*, pp. 91ff.

[111] It was *puritas cordis*, along with *tranquillitas* and *stabilitas*, which expressed in Cassian the sense of Evagrian *apatheia* (Lorie, *op. cit.*, pp. 125–126; see *Conf.* 1:7). For Cassian, *tranquillitas*, *stabilitas*, and *puritas* are used to express the perfection of *askesis*, where ascetic perfection and discernment of spirits are closely associated.

[112] *Conf.* 9:2.

[113] See part 2 in Chapter 1.

[114] Cf. *Inst.* 2:14, 3:2, 2:12; *Conf.* 9:5–6.

CONTROL OF THOUGHTS, FEELINGS, AND PASSIONS

By the power of the Holy Spirit, God's children can bear much fruit. As we are reminded in the Gospels, "by their fruits shall you know them" (Mt.7:16). In St. Paul we hear that among the fruits[115] of the Holy Spirit are "love, joy, peace, patience, . . . and self-control."[116] Origen appreciates the need of self-control, especially in the perfection of prayer.[117] Similarly, Evagrius realizes that in order to grow in the spiritual life, a prerequisite was the careful monitoring of one's inner impulses and thoughts;[118] the monk from Pontus is aware of the influence on prayer of angry thoughts and passionate remembrances.[119] For Cassian, it is important to realize what the mind can and cannot do with regard to the state of its thoughts, for as he says, "it is impossible for the mind not to be approached by thoughts, but it is in the power of every earnest man either to admit them or to reject them."[120] He is aware of the importance of thought control in the life of prayer and even suggests how it might be done: "wherefore a monk's whole attention should thus be fixed on one point, and the rise and circle of all his thoughts be vigorously restricted to it."[121] Because there exists the tendency for the mind in prayer to become only a toucher or taster of spiritual meanings jumping from one Scriptural passage to another because of the fluctuation of feelings, Cassian advocates self-control:

> It is then well for us before everything else to know how we can properly perform these spiritual offices, and *keep firm hold* of this particular verse which you have given us as a formula, so that the rise

---

[115] St. Paul does not refer to the works of the Spirit (as in the works of the flesh), but to the *fruits* of the Spirit. As a tree bears fruit, the Christian, in the Spirit, produces attitudes similar to God. The life of man in the Spirit is dependent on and united to the Spirit of God, like a blossom or fruit is dependent on the plant for its life. Self-control (*enkrateuesthai*, to exercise self-control, 1 Cor.9:25, 7:9; see SHI, pp. 182, 273) often refers to sexual comportment (1 Cor. 7:9), but in general, it refers to the control over any pure instinct, which enables us to resist the Spirit and to follow a life of the flesh.

[116] Gal. 5:22–23; see Origen, *On Prayer* 25:3.

[117] *On Prayer* 2:2; see 1 Cor. 7:5 and *Conf.* 17:20.

[118] *Praktikos*, 50.

[119] *Ibid.*, 23.

[120] *Conf.* 1:17.

[121] *Ibid.*, 24:6. There are elements here of hesychastic prayer.

and fall of our feelings may not be in a state of fluctuation from their own lightness, but may lie under *our own control.*[122]

Besides thoughts and feelings which Cassian understands as needing control, there are also passions. Cassian follows Evagrius in realizing the adverse effects of the passions on prayer and understands the need for self-control. Evagrius is aware of the essential distinction between the demons and the passions, and that the passions are accustomed to be stirred up by the senses.[123] In fact, for Evagrius the demons may "act upon the thoughts through the passions, and on the passions through the senses or through the flesh."[124] For Evagrius, the demons (or evil spirits) have as their goal to keep each person from attaining *apatheia.*[125] Demons inspire evil thoughts, and when these are allowed to linger, they unleash passions in us and make the heart too heavy to focus on prayer.[126]

To help the mind and heart focus and gain control over passions, Cassian uses the repetition of a Scriptural verse.[127] The passions could be neither good nor indifferent. As the result of sin, the soul[128] has been cloaked with various passions and it is the aim of *praxis* to strip the soul of these, for

> the ability to pray is evidence of the great progress we have made in the destruction of that screen which we have built up around the divine kernel and behind which there is hidden our true self which[129] "addresses God most familiarly as its own Father."[130]

---

[122] *Ibid.*, 10:13. Emphasis mine.

[123] *Praktikos*, 38 and 35.

[124] "*Évagre le Pontique*" by Antoine et Claire Guillaumont, DSAM 3 (1954), 203. See also *Chapters on Prayer*, 46.

[125] Driscoll, *op. cit.*, p. 38. *Apatheia* is Evagrius' more usual term for the controlling of the passions.

[126] *Ibid.*, 95.

[127] *Conf.*10:10.

[128] The soul is by nature the image of God. The seeds of all the virtues are latent in us from the start, and it is they that constitute the image of God in the soul, which sin has defaced but not destroyed. See footnote #26 in Chapter 1.

[129] *Conf.* 9:18.

[130] "*John Cassian*" by Peter Munz, JEH 11 (1960), 14.

These passions are habits of the mind or behavior, and the process of undoing is a gradual one. It is the use of control under the guidance of discretion,[131] which Cassian understands as leading to gradual control of passions. The discerned control of early faults allows for later ones to be checked[132] and nurtures a God-centered internal disposition for prayer.

---

[131] *Discretio* is an effect of growth in prayer, for as prayer matures, discretion helps to moderate excesses where moderation is not the *discretio* itself but only its first fruit (see *Discretio* by Dingjan, *op. cit.*, p. 74).

[132] *Conf.* 5:10.

CHAPTER 3

EFFECTS OF PRAYER

Eastern Christian writers learned that the deification of the Christian is his participation in the glory of Christ and culminates in an experience analogous to that of the Apostles on Tabor. It was this light that the early Fathers experienced as the enveloping energies of the Son and the Spirit assimilating them into divinized beings, one with the Father in Jesus through His Spirit. It was the illumination of the Holy Spirit from this light which allowed for the expression of the effects of prayer. For Cassian it is only by purity of soul and by means of the "illumination of the Holy Spirit"[1] that one obtains pure prayer or contemplation, and he understands growth in the virtues as leading to purity of soul by means of discerned growth through prayer. A definite practical criterion by which to discern true prayer is the fruit it bears,[2] for as Jesus Himself said, "without me you can do nothing."[3]

1. *DISCRETION AND SPIRITUAL DIRECTION*

Although we appreciate the importance of a sound education in academic fundamentals, we are often reluctant to deal with spiritual fundamentals and hesitant at best in seeking spiritual direction to correct this deficiency. The works of Cassian speak to a solution of these needs through two effects of growth in prayer: (1) discretion and (2) spiritual direction.

---

[1] *Conf.* 14:9. Cassian reinforces the words of Abbot Isaac in *Conf.* 9:8.
[2] Cf. Mt. 7:16.
[3] Cf. Jn. 15:5; *Inst.* 12:9, *Conf.* 3:16.

DISCRETION

In the process of deification, Cassian emphasizes the importance of charity and purity of heart to reach the end of the spiritual journey, which is contemplation or the Kingdom of God: ". . . according to the measure of its purity . . . each mind is both raised and moulded in its prayer."[4] It is the use of control under the guidance of discretion which Cassian understands as leading to the gradual control of passions. As Dingjan mentions, discretion is an effect of growth in prayer, for as prayer matures discretion helps to moderate excesses where moderation is not the discretion itself but only its first fruit.[5] For Cassian, there is the need

> to *restrain* every moment of anger and *moderate* it *under the direction of discretion* . . . a wise man, by the ripeness of his counsel and moderation little by little diminishes it, and gets rid of it.[6]

Since the "reasonable measure by which one happens to dominate the passions, instead of setting-off an even greater disorder, is precisely the object of *discretio*,"[7] Cassian understands discretion as strengthening prayer.[8]

Cassian insists that a fault responsible for the downfall of otherwise good and holy monks is the lack of discretion. The word "discretion" for Desert Fathers has had three aspects: the discernment of spirits, the discernment of thoughts, the principle of the correct measure of action; all three aspects presupposed as a foundation the discernment of good and evil of which they were the development.[9] From biblical discernment of spirits there gradually emerged the idea of discretion as a needed virtue for growth in prayer. If there is a relationship for Cassian between discretion and conforming to the image of God, it pertains to the measure of purity of the soul. In the dynamic journey from image into likeness, the process of discernment through prayer is indispensable

---

[4] *Conf.* 10:6. See also 1:4, 5, 8.

[5] Dingjan, *op. cit.*, p. 74.

[6] *Conf.* 16:27. Emphasis mine. Note also 2:16.

[7] Dingjan, *op. cit.*, p. 46.

[8] Cf. *Inst.* 5:9; *Conf.* 2:4.

[9] Dingjan, *op. cit.*, p. 13. Cassian "appears to be the first who expressed the idea of measure by the term *discretio*."

for growth in purity of soul. It was through the basic and common need to distinguish between good and evil spirits that the Desert Fathers strove for a quality of discernment which allowed them to listen in prayer to the voice of God within them in their desire to follow Christ.

There is more than discernment of the good and the evil thought, of the good or evil intention: the important thing finally is the good and the right realization of that which one has recognized as just. Often in effect the devil dresses up as an angel of light, suggesting to us good thoughts; one only unmasks him by the *discretio* in the works, in avoiding the excessiveness, the lack of equilibrium toward which he pushes us.[10]

As Cassian relates from the blessed Antony, discretion is the charism of proper judgment, which helps one avoid the sin of excess in any undertaking:

> ... discretion alone was wanting, and allowed them not to continue even to the end. Nor can any other reason for their falling off be discovered except that as they were not sufficiently instructed by their elders they could not obtain judgment and discretion, which passing by excess on either side, teaches a monk always to walk *along the royal road*, and does not suffer him to be puffed up on the right hand of virtue, i.e., from excess of zeal to transgress the bounds of due moderation in foolish presumption, nor allows him to be enamoured of slackness and turn aside to the vices on the left hand, i.e., under pretext of controlling the body, to grow slack with the opposite spirit of luke-warmness.[11]

The importance for Cassian of the virtue of discretion and the concern he has when it is not present is illustrated in a practical way through numerous stories[12] concerning deceived holy men of the desert; in many of these stories the devil takes on the appearance of an angel of light[13] while manifesting the ultimate in deceit, especially during the inner struggle.[14]

---

[10] *Ibid.*, p. 250.

[11] *Conf.* 2:2. Emphasis mine. Note *Conf.* 10:11. Cassian will be one of the first to employ the image of the "royal road" about discretion.

[12] *Ibid.*, 2:5, 7, 8.

[13] See footnotes #63–64 in Chapter 2.

[14] Cf. *Conf.* 10:10.

Cassian, realist as he was, recognized himself as a beginner,[15] and realized that even the most proficient of the holy men of the desert are vulnerable to the onslaught of the demonic. They are particularly vulnerable because they have achieved a peaceful disposition in prayer and remarkable virtue. As Abba Poemen relates, no matter how holy the person, vigilance is demanded at every moment, so cunning and clever are the evil spirits: "Vigilance, self-knowledge and *diakrisis*; these are the guides of the soul."[16]

Diakrisis, the basic discernment of good and evil, provides a gradual growing inner awareness and the "seeing clearly into oneself"; the "knowledge of Christ needs not a dialectical soul, but a seeing soul; knowledge due to study one can possess even without being pure."[17] In order to make use of the gift of discernment received through the Spirit, St. Antony says "much prayer and asceticism is needed."[18] The thirty-five year ascetical experience of Antony allows him to discern continually the various kinds of evil spirits and the proper remedy against each. This continuous and dynamic movement through discernment of spirits toward God is our gradual conforming to the image of God, for as Evagrius admits, "the man who is progressing in the ascetic life diminishes the force of passion."[19] Cassian knew[20] that the soul, which develops in charity, becomes more and not less conscious of sin, for

> ... even saints, and, if we may so say, men who see, whose aim is the utmost perfection, cleverly detect in themselves even those things which the gaze of our mind being as it were darkened cannot see.[21]

According to Cassian, the growing awareness of sin necessitated, especially for those who were thirsting for instruction in perfection, the need to grow in the process of discernment:

---

[15] *Inst.* 12:24.

[16] Fr. Dingjan, O.S.B., "La discretion dans les apophtegmes des Peres," *Angelicum* 39 (1962), 408. Emphasis mine.

[17] Hausherr, *Spiritual Direction in the Early Christian East, op. cit.*, pp. 86, 89.

[18] *Vita Antonii*, #22.

[19] *Praktikos*, 87. See also *Praktikos*, 89.

[20] Chadwick, *op. cit.*, p. 54.

[21] *Conf.* 23:6. See also 23:16.

... that we may conveniently recognize the signs by which we can discern and detect it, that when the roots of this passion are laid bare and brought to the surface, and seen and traced out with ocular demonstration, they may be the more easily plucked out and avoided.[22]

Cassian uses the idea of progressing in the ascetic life with gradual growth in the image of God and integrates it with the importance of discernment by speaking of a "fourfold method of discrimination" by which we "constantly search all the inner chambers of our hearts, and trace out the footsteps of whatever enters into them with the closest investigation,"[23] The process of discernment begins when there are inner movements and the question arises: Is the Lord revealing Himself and if so what is He saying? Spiritual growth for Cassian is intimately connected with the examination of whatever enters the heart to see or discern whether it has been purified.[24] The New Testament recognizes the charisma of discernment of spirits and Cassian utilizes Scripture, in this case 1 Cor. 12:8–11,[25] to highlight the fact that

... unless a monk has pursued it with all zeal, and secured a power of discerning with unerring judgment the spirits that rise up in him, he is sure to go wrong, as if in the darkness of night and dense blackness, and not merely to fall down dangerous pits and precipices, but also to make frequent mistakes in matters that are plain and straightforward.[26]

If one is contemplating Scripture, it is necessary to let the Scriptures be themselves and to listen to them and to ask our Lord to reveal Himself

---

[22] *Inst.* 12:29.

[23] *Conf.* 1:22.

[24] *Ibid.*, 1:20. Note that St. Thomas defines "discernment of spirits" as the ability "to display what it belongs to God alone to know . . . future contingencies . . . and also the secrets of the heart." (cf. *Summae Theologicae* [1a.2ae, III,4], Vol. 30, New York, 1972, p. 139).

[25] One may have the gift of preaching with wisdom given him by the Spirit; another may have the gift of preaching instruction given him by the same Spirit; and another the gift of faith given by the same Spirit; another again the gift of healing, through this one Spirit; one, the power of miracles; another, prophecy; another, the gift of recognizing spirits; another, the gift of tongues, and another, the ability to interpret them. All these are the work of one and the same Spirit, who distributes different gifts to different people just as he chooses.

[26] *Conf.* 2:1. Note also 1 Jn. 4:1.

while we are listening to these words. For Cassian, it is through listening in prayer that one enters into a relationship with the living Lord, and hence begins the dynamic process of conforming oneself according to the Image through discernment of spirits in the silence of one's heart.

It is in the silence of the heart that we come to realize that the peak of human freedom is unselfish love, as Jesus Himself said: "You must love the Lord your God with all your heart, with all your soul, and with all your mind."[27] Fundamental to the spiritual life for Cassian and motivated by the love of God is a continual asceticism, which expands one's capacity for His love. This willingness to live not according to the flesh but according to the Spirit in true humility draws one by discernment of spirits through prayer from imaginative and discursive meditation about God, to an awareness of His presence independent of imagination and reason. For Cassian

> ... true discretion ... is only secured by true humility ... For a man cannot possibly be deceived, who lives not by his own judgment but according to the example of the elders, nor will our crafty foe be able to abuse the ignorance of one who is not accustomed from false modesty to conceal all the thoughts which rise in his heart, but either checks them or suffers them to remain, in accordance with the ripened judgment of the elders. For a wrong thought is enfeebled at the moment that it is discovered: and even before the sentence of discretion has been given, the foul serpent is by the power of confession dragged out, so to speak, from his dark underground cavern, and in some sense shown up and sent away in disgrace. For evil thoughts will hold sway in us just so long as they are in the heart.[28]

Because excesses in fasting, gluttony, and vigils must all be moderated, Cassian insists that

> We ought then with all our might to strive for the virtue of discretion by the power of humility, as it will keep us uninjured by either extreme, for there is an old saying: extremes meet ... as the apostle says "with the arms of righteousness on the right hand and on the

---

[27] Cf. Mt. 23:37.
[28] *Conf.* 2:10.

left,"[29] we pass on with due moderation, and walk between the two extremes, under the guidance of discretion.[30]

FASTING?

Cassian is a realist and knows that lack of self-worth leads to lack of self-control. He knows the importance of first getting the body under control[31] and then allowing for a gradual eradication of the basic egotistical instincts that attach us to the world.[32] Nevertheless, all the renouncements of asceticism are useless, Cassian says, if one does not possess the charity[33] that St. Paul speaks of in 1 Cor. 13:3. Such impulses, guided by true discernment, toward purity of heart and apostolic love[34] come first from God, and it is the Holy Spirit who leads one into the deeper Christian values of fasting. Fasting can aid in sensitizing each person to listen and grow in openness to the Holy Spirit in turning oneself to God with a more sensitive heart to love and serve one's neighbor. Cassian is aware of the need for growth in a God-centered inner disposition to avoid an "unfruitful fast,"[35] for as he admits,

> perfection is not arrived at simply by self-denial, and the giving up of all our goods, and the casting away of honors, unless there is that charity, the details of which the Apostle describes, which consists in purity of heart alone[36] . . . fasting is certainly not considered by the Lord as a thing that is good in its own nature, because it becomes good and well-pleasing to God not by itself but by other works, and again from the surrounding circumstances it may be regarded as not merely vain but actually hateful, as the Lord says: "When they fast I will not hear their prayers" (Jer.14:12).[37]

---

[29] Cf. 2 Cor. 6:7.

[30] *Conf.* 2:16.

[31] *Ibid.*, 2:2.

[32] *Inst.* 5:34.

[33] *Conf.* 1:6, 11; 1 Cor. 13:3 (If I give away all that I possess, piece by piece, and if I even let them take my body to burn it, but am without love [agape], it will do me no good whatever).

[34] *Ibid.*, 21:17.

[35] *Ibid.*, 9:34; see Is. 58:6–7.

[36] *Ibid.*,1:6.

[37] *Ibid.*, 21:14.

Fasting is fundamentally an act of offering oneself to God through the sacrifice of a humble and contrite heart. Ultimately, the person must confront God; fasting is only a means by which the person can be led through discerned experience to realize more fully his dependence on and relationship to God. It is fasting which should lead to practice of the virtues such as patience and love.[38] Yet, as Cassian would admit, asceticism without discernment leaves an individual far from God. It is the quality of discernment which enables one to hear in his heart the voice of God above all the other voices which clamor for his attention. Just as each person progresses by divine grace to a higher ontological likeness to God, this purification of heart is gradual through the process of discernment.

Purity and peace of heart, for Cassian, resided in one's own control,[39] and their growth is helped by the perfection of patience;[40] in fact, as he admits, "patience had to be maintained, not in words, but in inward tranquillity of heart."[41] Cassian admits that growth in patience nurtures growth in prayer and a "largeness of heart."[42]

SPIRITUAL FRIENDSHIP?

Evagrius understands "enlargement of the heart" as a direct consequence of growth in contemplation.[43] As Evagrius admits, "He who has enlarged his heart by purity will understand the reasons of God, reasons which concern *praktike* and natural contemplation and theology."[44] Cassian appreciates this and insists that "there are plenty of roads to God,"[45] so any man or woman has a chance for perfection. The observation of rules or outward acts is important for him, but what really matters is what happens inwardly, the "state" of the soul; the

---

[38] *Ibid.*, 21:15.

[39] *Inst.* 8:17 and *Conf.* 1:6–7.

[40] *Conf.* 18:16.

[41] *Ibid.*, 16:22.

[42] *Ibid.*, 16:3, 5, 6, 22, 27, 28. Note Ps. 119:32 and 1 Kings 4:29. As A. Fiske points out, "perhaps magnanimity best describes Cassian's ideal friend, . . . a humble and patient magnanimity" (see "*Cassian and Monastic Friendship*" by Mother A. Fiske, R.C.S.J., ABR 12,2 [1961] 199).

[43] *Ad Monachos* 135; see Driscoll, *op. cit.*, SA 104 (1991), 70.

[44] *In Prov.* 22:20; see *Schol. in Prov.* SC 340 (1987), 93–95.

[45] *Conf.* 14:6.

practical and theoretical aspects of the inward journey are inextricably mingled. Cassian recognizes that for growth in the spiritual life, especially for growth in prayer, there has to exist at least a desire for moral growth and receptivity to the Word of God. Cassian appreciates the suddenness in which this desire can take place.[46] As Chadwick says,

> The Egyptian way, or rather ways, of life had an ordered intention. Cassian needed to make his version of it more ordered than the original. You aim to know God. You must go into a community. Then you will live with others who have the same intention and the same aspiration. Over years in that community you must learn to practice prayer, and the moral life that is necessary to prayer.[47]

Cassian sees the importance of a common moral aim in community. This is a direct result of his growing appreciation of spiritual friendship;[48] a friendship as he experienced with Germanus in Bethlehem and then wanted to witness to in southern Gaul:

> . . . the full and perfect grace of friendship can only last among those who are perfect and of equal goodness, whose likemindedness and common purpose allows them either never, or at any rate hardly ever, to disagree, or to differ in those matters which concern their progress in the spiritual life.[49]

While Evagrius is "aware of a transition period between *praxis* and *theoria* in which these two support each other,"[50] Cassian sees this transition period as a bridge or state of prayer which is integrally supported by the memory of Holy Scripture, discernment, and the examples of others. It is the loving wise counsel and example of those in community which helps Cassian appreciate the concept of spiritual friendship. This friendship demands discretion and patient self-control, and is an indissoluble form of charity, an "apostolic" charity,[51] which in its perfected form is identified with God Himself.[52] Cassian appreciates

---

[46] *Ibid.*, 14:10.

[47] Luibheid, *op. cit.*, p. 5.

[48] *Conf.* 16:27, 28, 6.

[49] *Ibid.*, 16:5.

[50] Lorié, *op. cit.*, p. 131.

[51] *Conf.* 16:3, 5, 26–28. See Fiske, *op. cit.*, pp. 202–203.

[52] *Ibid.*, 16:14; 1 Jn.4:16, Rom. 8:26.

the need to grow in a perfected form of charity because he understands that

> true love set in order is that which, while it hates no one, yet loves some still more by virtue of the excellence of their virtues and merits . . . and loves these with a special affection; and which from this number makes a second choice through which are singled out some who are preferred to others in affection.[53]

His spiritual friendship is affective and presupposes a humble and patient magnanimity under the direction of discretion.[54]

Growth in the virtues, especially humility and patience, nurtures growth in faith-filled confidence during prayer, where one no longer depends on externals but now relies on a God-centered internal disposition, the "inner man," the inner life, the life of prayer.[55] It is the profundity and strength of the inner life which distinguishes each person, especially his life of prayer. Cassian places emphasis on the fact that Christ looks not only at external actions but also at the internal disposition created by means of prayer, the internal impulses and purity of the inner soul in which ideally "the inner man may not even silently be disturbed in itself at the blows of the outward man."[56]

True discernment is the guide to testing impulses, and Cassian tempers the dynamic process of moving from the image to the likeness of God with discernment. Perfection requires likeness, and the likeness is connected with the Spirit. Ultimately, the person must confront God, Who is the basic measuring rod for discernment of spirits.[57]

A barometer for Antony in the discernment of spirits is clearly the heart through which one enters into a relationship with all that exists: "when the heart rejoices, the countenance is cheerful; when it is in sorrow, the countenance is sad (Prov.15:13)."[58] It is only after thirty-five years of asceticism and personal struggle that Antony, transformed and

---

[53] *Ibid.*

[54] *Ibid.*, 16:6, 27, 28.

[55] *Ibid.*, 18:16.

[56] *Ibid.*, 16:22.

[57] Herbert Smith, S.J., *"Discernment of Spirits"* in RR 35 (1976), 438.

[58] Gregg, *op. cit.*, p. 81; see *Vita Antonii*, 67; also, Tomáš Špidlík, S.J., *"The Heart in Russian Spirituality,"* OCA 195 (1973), 372–374.

restored by the Spirit, gives his discourse on discernment.[59] Antony admits that the Holy Spirit's gift of discernment of spirits is the result of prayer and asceticism. Although personal experience is important, Cassian emphasizes not so much a spontaneous experience but a guided and controlled experience directed from the experience of the elders by the process of discernment with the Holy Spirit through prayer.[60] The practical experience of ascetical life is important for Cassian as well, but yet it is the Spirit that transforms and restores the person according to his own life, which images the life of the Son, who in turn is the life of the Father.

An element of asceticism, fasting, allows an individual to feel his dependence on God and can aid in sensitizing him to listen and grow in openness to the Holy Spirit in turning himself to God with a more sensitive heart to love and serve his neighbor. Yet, even as Cassian would admit, asceticism without discernment leaves an individual far from God. It is the quality of discernment, which enabled one to hear in his heart the voice of God above all the other voices, which clamored for his attention. Just as man progresses by divine grace to a higher ontological likeness to God, this conversion of heart is gradual through the process of discernment.

The importance of experience in the ascetical life through discernment of spirits and the dynamic internal movement of growing according to the image in Christlike virtues is very much evident in the spiritual writers. Cassian says that ". . . it is impossible for an impure soul (however earnestly it may devote itself to reading) to obtain spiritual knowledge."[61] He emphasizes that a certain internal disposition, based on Christlike humility, is necessary for this spiritual growth, for "humility . . . is the mistress of all virtues, it is the surest foundation of the heavenly building."[62] Here Cassian echoes the thought of Antony, who says that

> He (our Lord) not only taught, but also accomplished what he taught,
> so that everyone might hear when he spoke, and seeing as in an

---

[59] Joseph T. Lienhard, S.J., "*On 'Discernment of Spirits' in the Early Church,*" TS 41,3 (1980), 517; also, *Vita Antonii*, 22.

[60] Michel Olphe-Galliard, S.J., "*Vie contemplative et vie active d'après Cassien,*" RAM 16 (1935), 258; see *Conf.* 2:11.

[61] *Conf.* 14:14.

[62] *Ibid.*, 15:7.

image, receive from him the model for acting, hearing him say "Learn from me, for I am gentle and lowly in heart" (Mt.11:29). A more perfect instruction in virtue one could not find than that which the Lord typified in himself.[63]

For Cassian,[64] true discretion is only secured by true humility with, as Dingjan says, *discretio* seen as the extension of the discernment of good and evil up to the actions involved:

> He who doesn't know to moderate his *thoughts* and his *actions* in such a manner that he attains purity of heart, he who by the excess of his practices harms his health, strikes a blow at virtues or makes the passions increase, . . . that one doesn't have the "*discretio*," he doesn't know how to *discern* that which is good and true (and which consequently leads to God) from that which is bad, harmful and false and makes us a slave of the demon.[65]

According to Cassian, discernment is needed to progress in the perfection of prayer,[66] since spiritual direction nurtures the discernment for growth into a more focused disposition, which images forth the humility of Christ.[67] All aspects of discretion presupposed as a foundation the discernment of good and evil spirits, especially for growth in prayer. Cassian understood this discerned growth through prayer as being intimately connected with developing a God-centered internal disposition based on the virtues, especially humility. The importance of humility, especially in the process of discernment of spirits by means of prayer for Cassian, can be placed in a clearer perspective by seeing how some of the Desert Fathers viewed discernment.

---

[63] Gregg, *op. cit.*, p. 112; also, *Vita Antonii*, 13. A hundred years after Antony, Diadochus of Photike (400–486), like Cassian, will echo the importance of a humble heart for the dynamic growth in the interior prayer life of man and the conscious awareness of divine activity in the soul through the process of discernment of spirits (cf. E. Kadloubovsky & G.E.H. Palmer, *Writings from the Philokalia on Prayer of the Heart*, translation, Faber & Faber, London, 1979, pp. 251–252); also, *Vita*, 27, 30, 40, 67.

[64] *Conf.* 2:10.

[65] Dingjan, *Discretio, op. cit.*, p. 77. Emphasis mine.

[66] *Conf.* 10:9. Discernment for Cassian is in the context of prayer (cf. *Conf.* 10:6).

[67] *Inst.* 4:9.

SPIRITUAL DIRECTION

The Desert Fathers sought God, but in particular they sought him through a life of prayer, fasting, and silence. Through these three elements the Fathers as well as Cassian sought to obtain a purity of heart[68] by which they could see God in themselves and in the world around them. One of the dangers of living in society is that too much value is placed on the opinions of men. This is true today and certainly was a danger at the time of Cassian. In the desert this danger decreases, but it is still possible for a man to look at himself, as he would have others look at him. He wants to possess perfection because this makes him important, at least to himself. Yet, St. Paul reminds us of the importance of the stripping of self:

> You have stripped off your old behavior with your old self, and you have put on a new self which will progress towards true knowledge the more it is renewed in the image of its creator.[69]

The Desert Fathers were well aware of the many subtle ways of affirming oneself and in their sayings they provide many subtle warnings; for example, "if you see a young monk by his own will climbing up into heaven, take him by the foot and throw him to the ground, because what he is doing is not good for him";[70] and again, "do not dwell in a famous place, and do not become the disciple of a man with a great name. And do not lay any foundation when you build yourself a cell."[71] True perfection "is found only when one renounces the 'self' that seems to be the subject of perfection, and which 'has' or 'possesses' perfection."[72] Usually, one does not, however, simply decide to renounce one's self. One does it slowly, over a period of time through prayer, by renouncing one's will in individual things.

One way of renouncing one's will is to submit it to another. "Become not a lawgiver to thyself."[73] The beginner seeks from a spiritual guide rules for prayer, fasting, labor, etc., but guidance in the

---

[68] *Conf.* 1:6; see 1 Cor. 13:3.

[69] Cf. Col. 3:9–10. See also 1 Cor. 11:7 and *Conf.* 1:14.

[70] Thomas Merton, *The Wisdom of the Desert*, Norfolk, Conn., 1960, p. 47.

[71] *Ibid.*, p. 73.

[72] Thomas Merton, *"The Spiritual Father in the Desert Tradition,"* MS 5 (1968), 91.

[73] *Ibid.*, p. 103.

externals is by no means all of it. The stories and sayings of the Fathers abound with examples of the beginner who, because he has not yet achieved true perfection, has an erroneous idea of it. The beginner seeks something from his spiritual guide and the guide sets him right by giving him an answer that may be disconcerting. There are many examples from the Fathers of the Desert:

> A brother came to Abba Theodore and began to converse with him about things, which he had never yet put into practice. So the old man said to him, "You have not yet found a ship nor put your cargo aboard it and before you have sailed, you have already arrived at the city. Do the work first; then you will have the speed you are making now;"[74]

> A brother came to Scetis to visit Abba Moses and asked him for a word. The old man said to him, "Go, sit in your cell, and your cell will teach you everything."[75]

> Abbot Lot went to see Abba Joseph and said to him, "Abba, as far as I can I say my little office, I fast a little, I pray and meditate, I live in peace and as far as I can, I purify my thoughts. What else can I do?" Then the old man stood up and stretched his hands towards heaven. His fingers became like ten lamps of fire and he said to him, "If you will, you can become all flame."[76]

In these answers and others like them there is an effort to shake the seeker. There is a sudden twist, and a little more of reality is revealed and discerned. This is the essence of the spirituality of the Desert Fathers and the desert itself provides an image of it. It is a trackless waste, and as the beginner tries to discern his way, he keeps getting lost. He needs a higher power to tell him which way to turn. This is the context in which Cassian would emphasize discernment through prayer. Indeed, at one point fasting and prayer is the way, at another point solitude, and at still another compassion for one's fellow men. Sometimes the seeker discerns the direction from interior inspiration, but

---

[74] Benedicta Ward, SLG, *The Sayings of the Desert Fathers*. The Alphabetical Collection; translated, with a foreword by B. Ward, SLG and preface by Met. Anthony of Sourozh; Cistercian Publications Inc., Kalamazoo, Michigan, 1984, p. 75. See Theodore of Pherme, 9.

[75] *Ibid.*, p. 139. See Moses, 6.

[76] *Ibid.*, p. 103. See Joseph of Panephysis, 7.

more often he finds it through another who has himself found the way and whose purity of heart allows him to see, feel, or taste the will of God. As Evagrius says, ". . . do not set your heart on what seems good to you but rather what is pleasing to God when you pray. This will free you from disturbance and leave you occupied with thanksgiving in your prayer";[77] in this light, Cassian advocates that

> . . . it is well for us to consider this saying of the blessed Evangelist John, by which the ambiguity of this question is clearly solved: "This is," he says, "the confidence which we have in Him, that whatsoever we ask according to His will, He heareth us"(1 Jn.5:16). He bids us then have a full and undoubting confidence of the answer only in those things which are not for our own advantage or for temporal comforts, but are in conformity to the Lord's will. And we are also taught to put this into our prayers by the Lord's Prayer, where we say "Thy will be done," —*Thine* not ours.[78]

The answer to a question is for this particular seeker at this particular time. The answer is not just advice; it is meant to clear away some of the blindness that caused the question. In the future the seeker will be better able to discern by means of prayer the question and the interior movements of his soul for himself and thereby continue his spiritual journey. For Cassian, the virtue of discernment was most apt to lead us to where God is.[79] As I. Hausherr admits:

> in the gospel, discernment is called the eye and the lamp of the body, according to the Savior's statement: "The lamp of the body is the eye. It follows that if your eye is sound, your whole body will be filled with light. But if your eye is diseased, then your whole body will be all darkness" (Mt. 6:22–23).[80]

The interior moods, feelings, and movements are the "spirits" that must be sifted out, discerned, so one can recognize the Lord's call to him at the intimate core of one's being.

---

[77] *Chapters on Prayer*, 89.

[78] *Conf.* 9:34.

[79] *Ibid.*, 2:2.

[80] Hausherr's "Spiritual Direction . . . ," *op. cit.*, p. 79.

For the Fathers of the Desert, the soul matured in prayer only through discernment of spirits in battle.[81] In fact, as Hausherr emphasizes,[82] the gift of *diakrisis* so greatly surpasses all the others that it may even be the equivalent of a dispensation of age and of knowledge.[83]

The ordering of discernment of spirits to see and choose and do what God calls one to here and now is evident in the Desert Fathers from the beginning, although it becomes clearly articulated probably first of all in the writings of Evagrius. The Evagrian defense in fighting against the *logismoi* is connected with the traditional theory of discernment of spirits. According to Antoine and Claire Guillaumont, for Evagrius "one must know the psychological states tied to the action of the diverse spirits,"[84] for

> There are two peaceful states of the soul. The one arises from the natural basic energies of the soul and the other from the withdrawal of the demons. Humility together with compunction and tears, longing for the Infinite God and a boundless eagerness for toil—all these follow upon the first type. But it is vainglory along with pride that succeeds to the second type, and these lure the monk along as the other demons withdraw from him. The monk who preserves intact the territory of the first state will perceive with greater sensitivity the raids made upon it by the demons.[85]

And

> When you are praying against some evil thoughts and you find that you are freed from them readily, examine how this comes about lest you fall into some hidden trap, and by being deceived betray yourself.[86]

In his important work entitled the *Praktikos*, Evagrius never uses the term "discernment" (*diakrisis*), and for him the demons are not the imaginative personalities of Antony but the colorless personifications of the eight capital sins.[87]

---

[81] See B. Ward, *op. cit.*, pp. 87–88. Note John the Dwarf, 13.

[82] Hausherr's "Spiritual Direction . . . ," *op. cit.*, pp. 81–82.

[83] See B. Ward, *op. cit.*, p. 210. Note an Abba of Rome, 2.

[84] Antoine and Claire Guillaumont, "*Évagre le Pontique: Traite Pratique ou Le Moine,*" Tome 1, SC 170 (1971), 204.

[85] *Praktikos*, 57.

[86] *Chapters on Prayer*, 133.

[87] Lienhard, *op. cit.*, p. 522; also, *Praktikos*, 4, 6.

In the *Sayings of the Desert Fathers* or *Apophthegmata Patrum*, the ability to distinguish between spirits, designated by the term *diakrisis pneumaton*,[88] does not appear, while the term *diakrisis* and its cognates are found in a number of the sayings of the Fathers.[89] In the words of Antony: "some have afflicted their bodies by asceticism, but they lack "discernment" (*diakrisis*), and so they are far from God."[90] Discerning God's voice, however, did not mean so much to destroy one's passions as to understand, and, as Cassian admits, to gain control of them by discernment through prayer, and ultimately to be able to use temptations as an interior guide for the soul to grow in prayer.[91]

Antony sees discernment of spirits as a continuous and dynamic movement of the humble soul to its true nature in the image of God. He insisted that the only way to grow in discernment is through spiritual experience. In order to advance in the ability to discern spirits, one must grow in clarity within one's own spirit and prayer life. For Antony, as Cassian admits, those lacking the training provided by older men could in no way acquire this virtue of discretion which, avoiding extremes, teaches the monk to walk always on the royal road.[92]

For Cassian, it is nurturing the experience of humility by means of prayer which allows one to grow in spiritual self-knowledge through discernment. It is the confidence resulting from this experience which Cassian recognizes besides grace as helping growth in discernment. Faith-filled confidence[93] in prayer is always tempered for Cassian by humility and purity of conscience.[94]

Cassian echoes the humble thoughts of Antony[95] in advocating the importance of the spiritual advice of older men:

> Who then is so self-sufficient and blind as to dare to trust in his own judgment and discretion when the chosen vessel confesses that he had

---

[88] First used by St. Paul in 1 Cor. 12:10.

[89] Lienhard, *op. cit.*, p. 520; also, Dingjan, "La discretion dans les apophtegmes, . . ." *op. cit.*, p. 406.

[90] B. Ward, *op. cit.*, p. 3. See Anthony the Great, 8. Also, see p. 61 (Eulogius the Priest, 1) and p. 190 (Poemen, called the Sheperd, 170).

[91] *Ibid.*, p. 171 (note Poemen, 28) and p. 154 (note Nisterus, 2).

[92] *Conf.* 2:2.

[93] *Ibid.*, 9:32.

[94] *Ibid.*, 9:33.

[95] B. Ward, *op. cit.*, p. 2. See Anthony the Great, 6.

need of conference with his fellow apostles. Whence we clearly see
that the Lord does not Himself show the way of perfection to anyone
who having the opportunity of learning despises the teaching and
training of the Elders, paying no heed to that saying which ought most
carefully to be observed: "Ask thy father and he will show it to thee:
thine Elders and they will tell thee." (Dt.32:7)[96]

When Cassian mentions "elder" or "old" men it does not imply "old in
age" but in the spiritual life. In fact, he warns against the prestige of
years: ". . . we are not to follow in the steps or embrace the traditions
and advice of every old man whose head is covered with grey hairs, and
whose age is his sole claim to respect."[97]

In order to help develop comfortableness during the journey in
prayer, Cassian advocates the importance of a spiritual father (elder or
guide) who was to intercede and mediate God's grace for the directee.
The aim of the spiritual guide was to set in motion an interior dynamic.
This interior dynamic represented a change from what "one was" to
what "one could become."[98] Spiritual direction was a continuing process
used to develop an ongoing attitude; there was always more to
become.[99]

While he was to teach, the spiritual guide was also to help one renounce "self" so that one could be led to perfection in God; true perfection is found only when one renounces the "self," by slowly
renouncing one's will in individual things.[100] In his portrait of a true
spiritual guide, Cassian insists on the virtue of humility, which is
necessary for discernment.[101] A simple discussion with a spiritual guide
can lead to growth in humility, peace in one's prayer life, and inner
freedom from "confession."[102] The "confession" mentioned here is not

---

[96] *Conf.* 2:15.

[97] *Ibid.*, 2:13; see Hausherr's "Spiritual Direction . . . ," *op. cit.*, p. 188.

[98] As with Clement of Alexandria, who was preoccupied with man's becoming more
spiritual, and Origen's concern with man's completion found in his becoming an
untarnished image of God, Cassian believed that becoming more perfect in the spiritual
life involved growth in the virtues by means of prayer.

[99] Joseph J. Allen, "*The Inner Way: The Historical Tradition of Spiritual Direction*,"
SVTQ 35, 2–3 (1991), 257–270.

[100] Tomáš Špidlík, S.J., "La direzione spirituale nell'Oriente cristiano," *Vita consacrata*
16 (1980), 510.

[101] *Conf.* 2:10.

[102] *Ibid.*, 2:11.

a sacramental act as in our daily and strict sense, but an ascetical means of spiritual help in one's aspiration for spiritual perfection especially in prayer. As Hausherr says,

> A careful distinction should be made between two types of confession, the accusation of sins with a view to absolution, and the "revelation of thoughts" with a view to spiritual direction to be received.[103]

The directee opens his conscience to a spiritual guide, who is distinguished by prudence and experience in life, in the hope of receiving the spiritual direction, which the guide feels is needed.

Within the monastic life of the Christian East, spiritual guidance took place principally at the time of *exagoreusis*,[104] that is, during determined daily encounters between the spiritual guide and directee.[105] The direction or guidance was most spiritually edifying when the directee communicated to the spiritual guide all shortcomings. As St. Paul said: ". . . let a man examine himself . . ."[106] It was during this manifestation of thoughts that one developed the ability to guard the mind and heart, recalling 1 Pet. 5:8: "Be sober and watch well; the devil, who is your enemy, goes about roaring like a lion, to find his prey." For Cassian, there is always a striving need for realism and openness with one's spiritual guide; otherwise one will only be victimized and unable through God's grace in prayer to become more Christlike.[107]

2. *SPIRITUAL LIFE*

As we begin to experience the explosive growth of the computer age, temptations[108] become stronger to succumb to the enticements of

---

[103] Hausherr's "Spiritual Direction . . . ," *op. cit.*, p. 99.

[104] That is, manifestation of thoughts (*exagoreusis ton logismon*) or "the movement of spirits"—as distinct from purely sacramental confession which was made to only a priest.

[105] Tomáš Špidlík, "La direzione spirituale . . . ," *op. cit.*, p. 509.

[106] Cf. 1 Cor. 11:28.

[107] B. Ward, *op. cit.*, p. 32. See Amoun of Nitria, 3. Also, see *Conf.* 2:13, 23:11 and Rom. 7:23.

[108] See part 2 in Chapter 2.

computer capabilities[109] and neglect the practice of fundamentals. The computerization of society inundated with the drive toward immediate gratification has highlighted the need for some form of patience[110] and the ability to deal with the notoriously short attention span of many young Americans. Against a constant refrain that we are "dumbing-down the American educational system," there is the deep-seated realization that there is no substitute for "practice" and the development of fundamental skills. The growth process in the educational system as well as in the spiritual realm is like a marathon, not a sprint; maturity and confidence are developed and nurtured over the longhaul, where confidence without competence is short-lived. We expect terrifyingly little of today's students, and they are responding in kind; in fact, for society in general there exists a growing index of acceptance of lower standards. Like the growth process in mathematical development, maturity in the spiritual life is developed in stages *from* the more practical and external *to* the more theoretical and internal, while always keeping one's priorities right and in view.

In a world often obsessed with the outer (external) qualities of life, the works of John Cassian speak to the importance of the inner life[111] and the need to nourish an internal disposition, especially in prayer. For Cassian, there is a relationship between the "inner life" and prayer. "Growth in prayer,"[112] especially pure or contemplative prayer, is directly related by Cassian to the gradual transformation into the image and likeness of God.[113] It is this process of growth, this growth in perfection by way of prayer, which Cassian associates with the image and likeness of God. We imitate the saints who are those who were pliable in allowing the Holy Spirit to sanctify them as they grew in likeness to the Image who is Christ.

---

[109] In the area of mathematics, for example, computer technology can be used to entice the beginner into appreciating only "the answer" (or exterior result) while minimizing the importance of "the process" (or interior result) used to obtain it. It's a case of fool's gold: all velocity—no coherence.

[110] See part 1 in Chapter 2.

[111] Cf. *Conf.*, First Preface, 4.

[112] "Growth in prayer" for Cassian is conditioned by a *puritas cordis* and the mystical element is found in the *illuminatio sancti Spiritus* (cf. *Conf.* 14:9). Human endeavor in the study of Scripture is needed in the formation of the internal disposition, because grace does not as a rule presuppose human inertia and sloth, but the activity of the natural powers.

[113] See footnote #26 in Chapter 1; cf. *Conf.*10:1, 2, 3, 5, 6; 11:7, 9.

The principal intent of Cassian is that of forming above all the interior of the person.[114] Each person is transformed with Christ's help by means of prayer; this transformation is, however, gradual. The gradual controlling of one's passions is then followed by acquiring through prayer the needed virtues for perfection.[115] Because the spirituality of Cassian is theocentric, the transformation through prayer from image to likeness consists in the continual force of deification considered under two aspects: one an "active or practical" mode, and the other a "contemplative or theoretical" mode. The active mode is concerned with the practical exercise of virtue through discernment in prayer. It is in this active mode that one begins to develop a prayerful disposition with two characteristics: (1) a practical and optimistic view of the spiritual life and (2) a conscious understanding that spiritual growth needs continual nourishment.

PRACTICAL AND OPTIMISTIC VIEW

While in his later years he seemed to say that solitary life was not practical in spite of its theoretical excellence, Cassian nevertheless utilized the Evagrian preoccupation with the mind[116] in the practical aspects of prayer by emphasizing the importance of the condition of the mind before prayer.[117] In general, Cassian has a practical and optimistic view of the spiritual life in which the degree or level of prayer is not as important as the internal disposition before and during that prayer, for even at the lowest stage of prayer the soul can find itself inundated with an abundance of spiritual fervor and the experience of pure prayer:

> Et inde est, quod in qualibet mensura quis positus nonnumquam puras intentasque preces inuenitur emittere, quia et de illo primo et humili ordine, qui est supor recordatione futuri iudicii, is qui adhuc sub terroris est poena ac metu examinis constitutus *ita ad horam conpungitur, ut non minore spiritus alacritate de obsecrationis pinguedine repleatur, quam ille qui per puritatem cordis sui munificentias dei perlustrans atque percurrens ineffabili gaudio laetitiaque resoluitur.* Incipit enim secundum sententiam domini plus diligere, quia sibimet ampliora cognoscit indulta.[118]

---

[114] Cf. *Inst*. praef.

[115] Cf. *Conf.* 14:3. See part 3 in Chapter 2.

[116] Marsili, *op. cit.*, p. 53.

[117] Cf. *Conf.* 9:3.

[118] *Ibid.*, 9:15. Emphasis mine. See SC 54 (1958), 52–53.

If we reflect on the unity of this text, we see a dynamic relationship between two degrees of perfection in prayer and the practical words of Jesus. Discerning the structure of the text is prerequisite for any proper interpolation. Here the structure is framed by the verbs "is found to offer up" (inuenitur emittere), "is touched (by [contrition])" [conpungitur], "is filled (with)" [repleatur], "gazes on . . . considers" (perlustrans . . . percurrens), "is overcome (with)" [resoluitur], and "begins . . . to love" (incipit . . . diligere). While there is a definite sense of symmetry and practicality between the first and last lines, the core of the text is contained within the lines "it (the soul) senses this very moment deeply touched by contrition. From the abundance of its obsecration bursts forth the enthusiasm of the spirit, and it (the soul) is completely filled by it, not least that which, in the splendor of its purity, considers the good deeds of his God, and is overcome, in this sight, with joy and ineffable jubilation" (ita ad horam conpungitur . . . resoluitur). This core implies dynamic movement toward the possible experience of pure prayer ("joy and ineffable jubilation" [ineffabili gaudio laetitiaque] or "enthusiasm of the spirit" [spiritus alacritate]) once there is a beginning on the path toward a perfect state of purity. There is a corresponding and dynamic sense given to two sets of words in a two-level movement toward the experience of pure prayer: "is touched (by)" corresponds to and implies "gazes on and considers" on the first level of this movement while "is filled (with)" corresponds to and implies "is overcome (with)" on the second and higher level. Given the practical optimism of the beginning of this text and the importance that Cassian places on the internal disposition before and during prayer, the key words here pertain to the first level and the more inclusive term "is touched (by)," which highlights the significance of the last line citing the practical words of Jesus from Lk. 7:47.[119] Cassian is practical as well as dynamically optimistic, for the core of the text supports the practical words of Jesus and unfolds the optimistic view that even at the most elementary stage of one's prayer life, one may offer up "pure and devout prayers."

There is a growth process in prayer for Cassian and it is conditioned "little by little" from the state of the soul *before* prayer to its condition during prayer. As Cassian admits through Germanus:

---

[119] For this reason I tell you that her sins, her many sins, must have been forgiven her, or she would not have shown such great love. It is the man who is forgiven little who shows little love.

Quantum itaque opinio nostra sese habet, cuiuslibet artis seu disciplinae perfectio necesse est ut a quibusdam mollibus incipiens rudimentis facilioribus primum ac tenerrimis initiis inbuatur, *ut quodam rationabili lacte nutrita paulatim educataque succrescat atque ita ab imis ad summa sensim gradatimque conscendat*: quibus cum fuerit planiora principia et quodammodo ianuas adreptae professionis ingressa, ad penetralia quoque perfectionis et excelsa fastigia consequenter et absque labore perueniat. Nam quemadmodum pronuntiare puerorum quispiam simplices poterit copulas syllabarum, nisi prius elementorum characteres diligenter agnouerit? uel quomodo citatam legendi peritiam consequetur, qui breues et perangustas descriptiones nominum necdum est idoneus coniugare? qua autem ratione is qui peritia grammaticae disciplinae minus instructus est uel rhetoricam facundiam uel philosophicam scientiam consequetur?[120]

In this text we find a practical description of the growth process for training in perfection. The unity of the text is enclosed within a structure that describes this process. This structure is reinforced by the practical questions at the end of the text which support in a symmetrical fashion the first line. The core of the text is contained within the lines "thus nourished as with a fortified milk, the spirit grows, and rises little by little and by degrees from the most humble things to the loftiest" (*ut quodam rationabili lacte . . . conscendat*). If we reflect on the structure of the text, we see dynamic movement (inward and upward: "inmost shrine . . . lofty heights" [*penetralia . . . fastigia*]) and a relationship of completeness between the words "(must) begin" ([*necesse est*] *incipiens*), "(may) grow up" (*succrescat*) and "(will) arrive (at)" [*perueniat*]. Because of the concern for the condition of the soul in the process of gradual development from "before" to "during" prayer, the key word in the core is "to grow." The central idea for Cassian is the growth process in perfection, which is conditioned gradually ("little by little" [*paulatim*]) and "by degrees and step by step" (*sensim gradatimque*), toward arriving at continual recollection of God in prayer, by being "nourished."

CONTINUAL NOURISHMENT

The nourishment in the growth process for Cassian begins *before* the time of prayer, as he emphasizes by citing Abbot Isaac: "what we

---

[120] *Conf.* 10:8. Emphasis mine. See SC 54 (1958), 82–83.

would be found when at our prayers, that we ought to be before the time of prayer. For at the time of its prayers the mind cannot help being affected by its previous condition."[121] A gradual conforming to the image of God allows for the continual recollection of God where the elementary phases of prayer are in themselves states of recollection which help in praying through the activity of the memory.[122] In order to minimize any injurious occupation of the heart at the time of prayer, Cassian highlights the importance of the memory as nourishment in the growth process, especially its role in the quality of prayer[123] and its function to awaken conscience.[124]

The process of spiritual growth for Cassian involves practice because the perfection of every heart tends to continual and unbroken perseverance in prayer, for the sake of which we "practice all bodily labors as well as contrition of spirit."[125] According to G. I. Gargano, the memory of Holy Scripture (*memoria Scripturarum*) for Cassian offered

---

[121] *Ibid.*, 10:14.

[122] *Ibid.*, 9:3, 14–15, 25–26, 28, 34; 10:3–5, 10–11, 13.

[123] *Ibid.*, 14:13. Cassian makes a distinction in the spiritual realm between memorization (where there is a feeding on texts from Scripture [especially psalm verses], and a freedom to listen and allow God to act on the heart) and a search for discerned meaning or understanding (of the past, present, and future). Other authors may have used psalm verses for prayer, but Cassian was probably the first to articulate this use of Scripture to develop continuous prayer and eventually to minimize any gap between memory and understanding. Cassian admits through Abbot Isaac that "penetrated by the same sentiments in which the psalm has been sung or composed, we become, so to speak, the authors. . . . Instructed by our own experiences we are not really learning through hearsay but have a feeling for these sentiments as things that we have already seen; they absolutely do not have the effect of being committed to our memory, but we deliver them *from the bottom of our heart*, as if they were feelings naturally there and part of our being; it is not the reading which makes us *penetrate the meaning* of the words, but the acquired experience." (*Conf.* 10:11. Emphasis mine. See SC 54 [1958], 92–93).

[124] *Ibid.*, 9:14–15, 26, 28; 10:11. Cassian highlights the capacity of memory in those "troubled by the guilt of a humbled conscience" (*Conf.* 17:17) and in whom conscience bites, as it were, just like "the pricks of our sins smiting our heart" (*Conf.* 9:29).

[125] *Ibid.*, 9:2. For Cassian, growth in the virtues, especially humility and patience, nurtures growth in faith-filled confidence during prayer, where one no longer depends on externals but now relies on a God-centered internal disposition (cf. *Conf.* 18:16; see my article on "Patience . . . ," p.172). He understands confidence as part of the internal disposition which "flows from purity of conscience" and is always tempered by humility (cf. *Conf.* 9:33; see part one in Chapter 1).

the possibility to stabilize an order and succession in the *praxis*[126] of expulsion of vice and attainment of virtue, where the basic ingredients in this process toward a God-centered disposition for pure prayer are memory[127] filled with Scripture and good thoughts. The stabilization with the aid of psalm verses allowed for spiritual growth in purity of heart, internal peace, and eventually incessant prayer.[128]

Whether it was the community's ritual office,[129] lending itself to non-continuous prayer of the hours, or private personal prayer,[130] which could possibly lead to incessant prayer, Cassian recognized the importance of the example of Jesus and the use of Holy Scripture in prayer.[131] Personal silent prayer was at the very heart of common prayer, and the recitation of the Scriptures sustained private prayer; each Psalm in common prayer could be followed by a period of silent prayer, and private prayer could be nurtured by Holy Scripture. Nourishment from Scripture in the practice of prayer helped fuel the preparation and disposition of the soul for growth in the perfection of prayer and progress toward God:

> quisquis autem ex hoc proficiens statu non solum innocentiae simplicitatem possidet, sed etiam discretionis uirtute munitus uirulentorum serpentium exterminator effectus est habens contritum Satanan sub pedibus suis, et ad figuram rationabilis cerui mentis alacritate peruenit, pascetur in propheticis atque apostolicis montibus, id est excelsissimis eorum ac sublimissimis sacramentis. *Quorum iugi pascuo uegetatus omnes quoque psalmorum adfectus in se recipiens ita incipiet decantare, ut eos non tamquam a propheta conpositos,*

---

[126] Cf. *Conf.* 14:3; see "La 'Collatio XIV' di Giovanni Cassiano" by G. I. Gargano, Pontificio Ateneo Anselmiano, Rome, 1991, p. 43.

[127] While Evagrius warned that the memory must be controlled when we seek to pray (cf. *Chapters on Prayer*, 44–46), Cassian understood memory and one's thoughts as important parts of the spiritual struggle for growth in prayer. Nevertheless, Cassian believed that the "empty mind" might be dangerous (cf. *Conf.* 1:17; *Inst.* 2:15). An important means for Cassian to attain a sense of unity in prayer where the mind and heart are concentrated upon God was the utilization of memory with Holy Scripture (cf. *Conf.* 1:17, 14:10). The inner struggle to develop a spiritual turn to one's memory was gradual and effected a spiritual transformation which helped to establish a prayerful disposition. As R. Hutch admits, memory can open "a dimension of consciousness that transcends nature and thus shows spiritual purpose of life" (cf. "*Memory: Grist of the Spiritual Life*," SVTQ 32, 3 [1988], 226).

[128] See part 2 in Chapter 1.

[129] Cf. *Inst.* 2–3.

[130] Cf. *Conf.* 9–10.

[131] *Ibid.*, 10:13.

sed uelut a se editos quasi orationem propriam profunda cordis conpinctione depromat uel certe ad suam personam aestimet eos fuisse directos, eorumque sententias non tunc tantummodo per prophetam aut in propheta fuisse conpletas, sed in se cotidie geri inplerique cognoscat.[132]

In this text, we find a unified and systematic structure personalizing the experience of the rise in perfection of prayer. The structure is framed by Cassian with the words "advances" (*proficiens statu*), "becomes" (*effectus est*), "thriving (on)" [*uegetatus*], and "are fulfilled and carried out" (*geri inplerique*). The core of the text is symmetrically framed between practical beginning and ending statements, which refer to Old Testament passages[133] and personalize the growth experience in the perfection of prayer. This core is contained within the lines "invigorated by this food from which he is constantly being nourished, he becomes firmly convinced at this point of all the sentiments expressed in the psalms, that he recites them henceforth, not as having been composed by the prophet but as if he himself were the author, and as a personal prayer with the deepest compunction" (*quorum iugi pascuo uegetatus . . . depromat*). The key words here for Cassian are "to thrive (on)" [continually] so that one is able to grow spiritually by internalizing Scripture; to "thrive on" includes not only the process of receiving enough nourishment to sustain life by "feeding on" but also the more dynamic potential for quality growth. This includes a combined movement: to take (in)—to begin (to sing)—to utter (with). Cassian is practical in his analysis of the dynamic movement from advancing with "simplicity of innocence" and "discretion"[134] to becoming capable to thrive continually in this state and owning[135] the Psalms as one's own prayer.

---

[132] *Ibid.*, 10:11. Emphasis mine. See SC 54 (1958), 91–92.

[133] Ps. 104:18, Prov. 30:26.

[134] See Chapter 3 (part 1 above).

[135] In your spiritual journey of prayer are you an "owner" or just a "shopper"? The ownership here is of spiritual meanings experienced as the concomitant results of a steadfastness of heart and incessant prayer (cf. *Conf.* 10:14). Growth in prayer for Cassian is nurtured by patient self-control, discretion, and charity. Without patient self-control and discretion, the mind (in the "shopper" mode and often captive to a fluctuation of feelings) experiences in prayer a "lukewarmness" or "half-heartedness," as attested to in Rev. 3:15–16 ("I know all about you: how you are neither cold nor hot. I wish you were one or the other, but since you are neither, but only lukewarm, I will spit you out of my mouth"; cf. *Conf.* 4:12, 19). Growth in discretion allows for a focused development in prayer; however, focusing with a lack of self-control encourages the mind to experience a "lightness," an immediate temptation to jump from one scriptural text to another without spiritually savoring and listening for God's presence in any

   Prayer is dynamically cyclic (with an outward-inward-outward movement) for Cassian; it is prompted by Scripture which is taken in, allowed to affect the heart, and made one's own only to be fulfilled in one's daily life. The continual nourishment from Scripture helps to sustain the quality of spiritual growth and reduce the probability of an indiscernible experience.

---

particular text (cf. *Conf.* 10:13), and one becomes a "toucher or taster of spiritual meanings."

CHAPTER 4

JOURNEYS IN PRAYER

The spiritual journey for Cassian is a unique and gradual conforming to the image of God, the concomitant result of continual recollection of God and unceasing prayer.[1] His main concern in this journey is the goal of the ascetical life and its development within the context of a growing life of prayer.[2] Whether it is the community's ritual office,[3] lending itself to noncontinuous prayer of the hours, or private personal prayer,[4] which can possibly lead to incessant prayer,[5] Cassian recognizes that what counts most is the importance of the resulting internal disposition[6] and not a fixed form of words from prayer formulas. It is the malleable receptivity of the internal disposition which can be affected by the Holy Spirit or evil spirits for growth toward eternal life or death, respectively. Among the many spiritual journeys mentioned by Cassian, two journeys in prayer stand out, at least for this author.

1. *LUKEWARMNESS TO STEADFASTNESS*

Prayer is dynamically cyclic for Cassian and is prompted by Holy Scripture in a three-pronged movement: taken in, allowed to affect the heart, and made one's own only to be fulfilled in one's daily life. This movement has many analogies in everyday life, one of which is

---

[1] Cf. 1 Thess. 5:17.

[2] NJH, p. 193.

[3] Cf. *Inst.* 2–3.

[4] Cf. *Conf.* 9–10.

[5] See part 2 in Chapter 1.

[6] As one of the Apophthegmata puts it ". . . the Canaanite woman cries out, and she is heard (Mt.15); the woman with the issue of blood is silent, and she is called blessed (Lk.8); the pharisee speaks, and he is condemned (Mt.9); the publican does not open his mouth, and he is heard (Lk.18)" (cf. Benedicta Ward, SLG, *The Sayings of the Desert Fathers. The Alphabetical Collection*; translated, with a forward by B. Ward, SLG and preface by Met. Anthony of Sourozh [Kalamazoo: Cistercian Publications, 1984], pp. 57–58. See Epiphanius, 6).

71

experienced in any materialistic and permissive society and is commonly referred to as the "shopper—buyer—owner" mentality. A society held captive by this mentality is one in which moral and ethical values are minimized and people are repelled by materialism yet admit to being caught up in it; they say they feel under constant pressure, working too much and neglecting family life, yet they are ready to work even longer hours for more money; they say they are troubled by widespread poverty yet esteem wealth. In a society with increasing adultery and divorce rates, where young adults "live for the moment" in an atmosphere of moral indifference, there is a growing need for what Cassian would call "steadfastness of heart" with a moral compass and not the fickle lukewarmness of expediency; some moral compass is needed to guide the choice of careers, attitudes toward work, and patterns of spending.

While it is true that Cassian addressed a Western audience, there was still a process of adjustment that can be detected at many levels of his work. He promised in the *Institutes*, for example, to modify the customs of Egypt, placing less emphasis on elements which, "because of the severity of the climate, or owing to some difficulty or diversity of habits, is impossible in these countries, or hard and difficult."[7] This is certainly a practical and tactful ambiguity, with implications that could not be avoided. He referred rather pointedly to "the perfection of the Egyptians," and to their "rigorous teaching and practice," which was, he said, "beyond imitation."[8] He felt that he was dealing with men and women who, "because of their total neglect or half-hearted endeavor, are less acquainted with this degree of purity";[9] he thought there were few in his audience likely to have achieved such perfection, especially in prayer, that they were ready for the rigors of the solitary life, or liable to the dangers of spiritual pride.[10]

While Cassian deplores, but admits, the need to modify the teaching of the East, he states that

> if it should happen that anyone thinks these things impossible, or at least hard to bear, either for a person in his position, with his ambitions, or for a man anxious to contribute to the benefit, and share in the daily life, of others, then let him judge their value, not according to his own insignificant abilities, but rather according to the excellence and perfection of those who speak about such matters.[11]

[7] *Inst.*, preface.
[8] *Ibid.*, 3:1.
[9] *Ibid.*, 6:20.
[10] *Ibid.*, 12:24.
[11] *Conf.*, first preface, 6.

Cassian's assessment of the cenobitic life was linked with the spiritual weakness he thought he saw around him. Sheer publicity was to be the safeguard of virtue; the scrutiny of others would prevent backsliding and spur a monk on to greater austerity and observance.[12] Each person has social qualities that demand a social schooling.[13] This schooling would help provide appropriate discipline and nourish an interior disposition for prayer.

Progress in the spiritual life is for Cassian directly linked to growth in prayer, since perfection of the heart rests in "continual and unbroken perseverance in prayer."[14] Nevertheless, to grow in perfection means to grow in the virtues, especially humility and patience, and to gain control of one's thoughts, feelings, and passions. Without patient self-control[15] and discretion,[16] the mind experiences in prayer the "lukewarmness" or "half-heartedness" attested to by Jesus in Rev. 3:15–16[17] and languishes in a state of indecision, referred to hereafter as the "shopper" mode.

"SHOPPER" MODE

In the "shopper" mode we are often held captive to a fluctuation of feelings and find it difficult at best to make up our minds; indecision reigns in our hearts. In this state of indecision it is difficult at best to focus the mind and heart for any length of time, let alone pray. In order to begin to remedy this difficulty, Cassian appreciates the importance of a repetitive focus on prayer as well as neither fighting nor focusing on intruding thoughts.[18] Even manual labor has to be seen within proper limits of discerned control so that it remains an aid and not a hindrance to prayer.[19] The discerned control of early faults allows for later ones to

---

[12] Cf. *Inst.* 6:3; *Conf.* 1:20, 5:12.

[13] Cf. *Conf.* 5:4, 18:12.

[14] *Conf.* 9:2.

[15] See part 3 in Chapter 2. In general, self-control here refers to the control over any pure instinct, which enables us to resist the Holy Spirit and to follow a life of the flesh.

[16] See part 1 in Chapter 3.

[17] "I know all about you: how you are neither cold nor hot. I wish you were one or the other, but since you are neither, but only lukewarm, I will spit you out of my mouth"; Jesus condemns the state of self-satisfaction and lukewarmness (cf. *Conf.* 4:12, 19). According to Scripture (cf. 1 Cor. 3:2–3, 2:14–15; Gal. 6:1), as Cassian relates in *Conf.* 4:19, there are three kinds of souls: carnal, natural, and spiritual. Of these, the natural soul, which is characterized by lukewarmness, is the worst, for as Cassian relates: "We have often seen those who were cold and carnal, i.e., worldly men and heathen, attain spiritual warmth, but lukewarm and 'natural' men never."

[18] See part 2 in Chapter 1.

[19] Cf. *Inst.* 2:14, 3:2, 2:12; *Conf.* 9:5–6.

be checked[20] and nurtures a God-centered internal disposition for prayer.[21]

The ultimate goal, the *telos*, of the spiritual journey for Cassian is summarized in his first *Conference*: it is for the kingdom of heaven that we do all this. Nevertheless, the immediate end, the *scopos*, is purity of heart through spiritual growth in prayer, and this had to be obtained if only gradually in order for the *telos* ever to be realized. Cassian knew that "whatever helps lead us toward purity of heart we must practice with all our might, but whatever separates us from it we must shun as a harmful danger";[22] he knows that "each soul in prayer is stirred and shaped in accordance with the measure of its purity,"[23] and he understands discretion as strengthening prayer.[24]

Discipline demands discretion, for as Cassian relates from the blessed Antony, discretion is the charism of proper judgment which helps one avoid the sin of excess in any undertaking:

> ... *discretion* alone was wanting, and allowed them not to continue even to the end. Nor can any other reason for their falling off be discovered except that as they were not sufficiently instructed by their elders they could not obtain judgment and discretion, which passing by excess on either side, teaches a monk always to walk along the *royal road*, and does not suffer him to be puffed up on the right hand of virtue, i.e., from excess of zeal to transgress the bounds of due moderation in foolish presumption, nor allows him to be enamored of slackness and turn aside to the vices on the left hand, i.e., under pretext of controlling the body, to grow slack with the opposite spirit of *lukewarmness*.[25]

It is the lukewarm or half-hearted person, satiated and pleasure-ridden in mediocrity, who is spit out of the Lord's mouth.[26] Lack of discretion holds a person captive in this state of lukewarmness, for, as Cassian admits, "once he is infected by this miserable plague and is as it were unstrung by it, he can no longer of himself discern what is perfect nor learn from the admonitions of another."[27] However, growth in discretion

---

[20] Cf. *Conf.* 5:10.
[21] See part 3 in Chapter 2.
[22] *Conf.* 1:3–5.
[23] *Ibid.*, 10:6.
[24] Cf. *Inst.* 5:9; *Conf.* 2:4.
[25] *Conf.* 2:2. Emphasis mine. Note also 4:12, 24:24. Cassian will be one of the first to employ the image of the "royal road" about discretion.
[26] *Ibid.*, 4:19. See Rev. 3:15–16.
[27] *Ibid.*

allows the heart to enter into a "buyer" mode and encounter not a lukewarmness but a "lightness" in spiritual feelings, where the heart is still unable to penetrate meaning and lives only on its superficial perimeter but now refuses to let go of God. Nevertheless, life on the heart's superficial perimeter necessitates careful examination of those spirits which affect one's conscience[28] and heightens the struggle with one's inner demons.

"BUYER" MODE

The "buyer" mode is characterized by a deliberate sense of calculation, which more often than not results in taking half measures but rarely amounts to a full commitment. The need for growth in discretion and examination[29] of conscience is paramount here, especially in dealing with self-delusion. The "buyer" conserves self-will,[30] while deluding himself into believing that he has gotten rid of it. This delusion is remarkably apparent in spiritual reading for as Cassian admits,

> when the mind has taken in the meaning of a passage in any Psalm, this insensibly slips away from it, and ignorantly and thoughtlessly it passes on to a text of some other Scripture. And when it has begun to consider this with itself, while it is still not thoroughly explored, the recollection of some other passage springs up, and shuts out the consideration of the former subject. From this too it is transferred to some other, by the entrance of some fresh consideration, and *the soul*

---

[28] *Ibid.*, 1:20; see 1 Jn. 4:1. Note Inst. 5:9, 7:21,30, 8:4, 12:6,27; *Conf.* 2:13, 4:15, 9:8, 15, 19, 29, 33–34, 11:8, 13:12, 14:14, 17:17,25, 18:15, 19:3, 11–13, 16, 20:5, 7, 21:8, 22, 36, 23:17, 19.

[29] Cf. *Conf.* 19:11–12, 20:5; *Inst.* 12:27. Cassian understood confidence as being part of the internal disposition of true prayer which "flows from purity of conscience" and was always tempered by humility (*Conf.* 9:33); it was prayer in faith-filled confidence (*Conf.* 9:32) which was heard by God.

[30] According to Tomáš Špidlík, self-will is "the passionate movement that follows the *logismos*, the evil thought" [SHI, p. 256]. For the dangers of self-will, see Dorotheos of Gaza; for ex., *Dorotheos of Gaza: Discourses & Sayings*, trans. Eric P. Wheeler, CSS 33 (1977) 82–83, 87–89, 123–124, 239; for Dorotheos, "nothing helps men so much as to cut off self-will, for thereby a man prepares the way for nearly all the virtues . . . from this cutting off of self-will a man procures for himself tranquility and from tranquility he comes, with the help of God, to serene indifference" (p. 88) (see *apatheia*; Evagrius, *Praktikos* 57–68; on the whole, Evagrius understood *apatheia* not negatively but positively. It is not apathy in the modern sense of the word but the replacing of our sinful desires by a new and better energy from God. It refers to a state of the soul, a phase in the growth in prayer toward perfection [cf. *Praktikos* 64, and note the concept of hesychasm]).

always turns about from Psalm to Psalm and jumps from a passage in
the Gospels to read one in the Epistles, and from this passes on to the
prophetic writings, and thence is carried to some spiritual history, and
so it wanders about vaguely and uncertainly through the whole body
of the Scriptures, unable, as it may choose, either to reject or keep hold
of anything, or to finish anything by fully considering and examining
it, and so becomes only *a toucher or taster of spiritual meanings, not
an author and possessor of them.*[31]

Because there exists the tendency for the mind in prayer to become only
a toucher or taster of spiritual meanings jumping from one Scriptural
passage to another because of the fluctuation of feelings, Cassian
advocated self-control "so that the rise and fall of our feelings may not
be in a state of fluctuation from their own *lightness*, but may lie under
our own control."[32]

While being able to deal with a fluctuation of feelings was important
for Cassian, it paled in significance to the self-control of passions. The
passions were habits of the mind or behavior, and the process of undoing
was a gradual one.[33] Cassian was a realist and knew the importance of
first getting the body under control[34] and then allowing for a gradual
eradication of the basic egotistical instincts that attach us to the world.[35]
He understood that it was important to control the passions before trying
to destroy them,[36] especially if the inner spiritual struggle was to be
minimized and incessant prayer was to be nurtured.

---

[31] *Conf.* 10:13. Emphasis mine.

[32] *Ibid.* Emphasis mine.

[33] For Cassian, there exists an order in the process of undoing passions, especially when
it concerns habits of the mind or behavior. There is a growth process in knowledge for
Cassian, from the practical to the spiritual (cf. *Conf.* 14:9); the practice of prayer can
proceed to unceasing prayer. Likewise, the growth in discretion allows for control of
improper behavior and leads to the control of improper thoughts; as Cassian says, "if a
man is not able to control passions, which are openly manifest and are but small, how
will he be able with temperate discretion to fight against those which are secret, and
excite him, when none are there to see?" (*Inst.* 5:20). Unlike the mentality of a
generation ago when the social and ethical preoccupation was with behavior, now there
is a growing awareness of an "ist-mentality," a preoccupation with thoughts which are,
for example, sexist or feminist, to mention a few. Nevertheless, for Cassian it is the
memory filled with Holy Scripture and good thoughts which aided growth in purity of
heart by means of prayer. He emphasizes in the *First Conference* and reiterated in the
tenth that each soul in its spiritual struggle is stirred and shaped during *the time of
prayer* in accordance with the measure of its purity. For Cassian, "the time of prayer"
and "incessant prayer" are not mutually exclusive expressions (see part 2 in Chapter 1).

[34] *Conf.* 2:2.

[35] Cf. *Inst.* 5:34.

[36] Cf. *Conf.* 14:3.

"OWNER" MODE

The inner spiritual struggle intensifies as a person's interior life of perseverance in prayer develops. As prayer matures, discretion helps to moderate excesses and nurture growth of virtues. The enemy does its best to attack the virtues created by a growing interior disposition centered on prayer and a person's hard labor and perseverance during prayer.[37]

It is growth in self-control which allows us to focus more completely and achieve a steadfastness of heart where we become not only a toucher or taster but also an "owner" of spiritual meanings. The "owner" mode here for Cassian is of spiritual meanings experienced as the concomitant symbiotic result of steadfastness of heart and incessant prayer. As Cassian says:

> There are three things that make a shifting *heart* steadfast: watchings, meditation, and prayer, diligence in which and constant attention to will produce steadfast firmness of mind. But this cannot be secured unless all cares and anxieties of this present life have been first got rid of by indefatigable persistence in work, dedicated not to avarice but to the sacred uses of the monastery, that we may thus be able to fulfill the Apostle's command: *"Pray without ceasing"* (1 Thess. 5:17).[38]

If there is a characterizing element of the "owner mode" for Cassian, it is the inner freedom experienced from the integration of "heart" and "prayer." Integration here for Cassian is facilitated by the examination[39] of conscience and measured by the depth of realized inner freedom; it is the conscience, which bites us,[40] that is our guide[41] and gives the surest proof of pardon.[42]

2. *SOLITUDE TO OPENNESS*

While he itemizes the distinction between abstinence and chastity, Cassian highlights the importance of the struggle with passions in the former and the love of purity in the latter. Nevertheless, it is the journey

---

[37] *Ibid.*, 2:13, 7:6, 9:2.
[38] *Ibid.*, 10:14. Emphasis mine.
[39] Cf. *Inst.* 12:27. Note footnote #29 above.
[40] Cf. *Conf.* 17:17, 9:29.
[41] *Ibid.*, 21:22.
[42] *Ibid.*, 20:5.

from the struggle with passions to the love of purity which interested Cassian the most; ironically, this seems to concern the 21ˢᵗ century man and woman the least, especially in a culture that would prefer to delude itself concerning the indisputable power and importance of sex. When one has to encourage schools to teach that the expected standard of human sexual activity is mutually faithful, monogamous, heterosexual relationships in the context of marriage, there is a definite problem of disorder in spiritual priorities. Disorder in sexuality is related to disorder in the spiritual life; even St. Paul admonishes to "never let your love for each other grow insincere, since love covers over many a sin" (1 Pet. 4:8). The dynamic here for Cassian in the spiritual life is even more fundamental, for it includes the tension between "solitude" and "openness of heart" in any spiritual journey of unselfish love.

SOLITUDE

Temptations are a part of all of our lives. How we deal with them tells us who we are, but more importantly who we will become. There is nothing more seductive in the spiritual life than that which entices us to deal with temptation alone, without asking God's help, let alone that of a spiritual guide. In an age which encourages youthful identification with the "Rambo syndrome," that invincible "mano-a-mano" self-defense ideal, the transference of this worldly, arrogant pride to the spiritual realm can lead to disaster, and in the absence of the recollection of God, temptation cannot be far behind.[43] The epitome of this kind of seduction, centered on pride, is the transition from any self-induced solitude of one's heart to an ego-centered state of secrecy where one becomes completely preoccupied with self; this solitude is normally created in the demon's favorite domain, the desert within, and the continued seduction and constant promise of peace in a vaster solitude.[44]

Solitude is the furnace in which one's transformation into the image of God takes place. It is all alone in the solitude of one's heart that temptation happens—temptation, that unique and lonely experience, which permeates the journey in prayer.[45] Surrender to temptation, more often than not, leaves an individual vulnerable to a chain reaction of passions, as Cassian relates through the words of Theonas:

---

[43] *Ibid.*, 7:24, 8:19.
[44] *Ibid.*, 24:19.
[45] See part 2 in Chapter 2.

> We should realize that we must not be purified of a given vice merely because it preoccupies our thoughts with its own disturbances, but because it is not content to hold sway alone without the company of others, and once a group of more cruel vices has been admitted they ravage the mind that is subject to them and hold it captive in manifold ways . . . the whole multitude of the vices are joined together as one, and thus each vice, even if it begins to flourish in us by itself, furnishes the possibility of growth to others.[46]

For Cassian, it is important to control the passions before trying to destroy them.[47] This is more easily accomplished by dealing with individual passions as they occur rather than the conglomerate nature of the vices.[48] As K. Russell points out, "an individual may focus on one or the other vice, but the goal, Cassian emphasizes, is to stop the chain reaction"[49] of vices, for it is through repeated failures in succumbing to deception that one is led to a spirit of lukewarmness[50] followed by an unwillingness to disclose one's vulnerability, and eventually to a self-preoccupied state of solitude or emptiness in the spiritual journey. This kind of solitude, like undesirable silence,[51] is not good or evil in itself, but functional for good or for evil.[52]

The inclination to interior (or spiritual) solitude, like good character, begins early in life. Good character arises from the repetition of many small acts, and begins early in youth to establish a moral disposition reinforced by the habit of good behavior. So too, in the spiritual journey the inclination to God-invited solitude presupposes an existing disposition of comfortableness with external silence and, if not accompanied by the virtue of discretion, masks a slippery slope to self-deception. As Cassian admits,[53] "if a man is not able to control passions, which are openly manifest and are small, how will he be able with temperate discretion to fight against those which are secret and excite him when none are there to see?" The interior moods, feelings, and movements are the "spirits" that must be sifted out, discerned, so one can recognize the Lord's call at the intimate core of one's being.[54] The seed of spiritual growth lies in one's inner turning to God. There must

---

[46] *Conf.* 22:3.

[47] *Ibid.*, 14:3.

[48] *Ibid.*, 22:3.

[49] "*John Cassian on a Delicate Subject*" by Kenneth Russell, CS 27 (1992) 7.

[50] See part 1 in this chapter.

[51] Cf. Wathen, pp. 122–128.

[52] See part 2 in Chapter 1.

[53] *Inst.* 5:20; see footnote #107 in Chapter 2.

[54] Cf. Mt. 6:22–23; note *Conf.* 2:2.

exist a sensitivity to God's voice within as well as an interior awareness of evil.[55]

The lack of sensitivity to God's voice within allows a state of solitude to degenerate into proud silence[56] and indifference vis-à-vis evil. As Cassian says,[57] "we pray within our chamber, when, removing our hearts inwardly from the din of all thoughts and anxieties, we disclose our prayers in secret and in closest intercourse to the Lord." Indifference is functionally for evil when there exists a coldness, a tolerance for evil, and eventually a distaste for good; spiritually unprofitable anger soon follows where "God's righteousness is never served."[58]

The existence of sensitivity to God's voice within allows for an indifference that is functionally for good, where solitude is elevated, completed, or intensified by silence on all levels of our being: physical, psychological, and spiritual. This sensitivity includes the capability of being conscience-stricken while not hardening one's heart so that it can be touched or softened by the advances of one's neighbor.[59] Here, as Cassian admits, there is purity of heart and the capacity to experience a sense of shame, a painful emotion excited by a consciousness of guilt; Teilhard called it "passionate indifference," a heart-felt sensitivity and openness in discerning God's will in one's life.

For Cassian, discernment is needed to progress in the perfection of prayer,[60] since spiritual direction nurtures the discernment for growth into a more focused disposition, which images forth the humility of Christ.[61] Nurturing the experience of humility by means of prayer allows one to grow in spiritual self-knowledge through discernment. It is the confidence resulting from this experience which he recognizes, besides grace, as helping growth in discernment. Faith-filled confidence[62] in prayer is always tempered for Cassian by humility and purity of conscience[63] and leads to an inner freedom of openness in the spiritual

---

[55] Cf. *Conf.* 13:10; see *nepsis* in SHI (p. 243) and 1 Pet. 5:8. Note that attention, *prosoche*, is the mother of prayer, *proseuche* (see I. Hausherr, "*La methode d'oraison hesychaste.*" OC [1927], 118–134).

[56] Cf. Wathen, *op. cit.*, p. 123.

[57] *Conf.* 9:35; Mt. 6:6; see footnote #53 in Chapter 1.

[58] James 1:20; *Inst.* 8:1.

[59] Cf. *Inst.* 12:27.

[60] Cf. *Conf.* 10:9.

[61] Cf. *Inst.* 4:9.

[62] *Conf.* 9:32.

[63] *Ibid.* 9:33.

life,[64] an openness reflecting our Lord's words: "Father, into your hands I commit my spirit."[65]

OPENNESS OF HEART

A person becomes the desires that he or she entertains. He creates the world around him, at least the world that is important to him by the thoughts that he values. For Cassian, in any spiritual journey, there is growth in comfortableness with spiritual thoughts, not a "dislike of spiritual talk" where in conversation one's eyes cannot be "fixed on one spot," but the "gaze wanders blankly about here and there," and the "eyes shift hither and thither."[66] Discipline over one's thoughts so that they are all submitted to the presence and the love of Christ becomes the means for any entrance into true freedom. Such freedom can be won only by a constant battle over the powers of darkness that lie within the heart and the desire for making progress in the growth of virtues, for "when the desire of making progress ceases, there the danger of going back is present."[67] Nevertheless, progress here is measured by a discerned appreciation of one's vulnerability.

Vulnerability to any passion makes one ripe for deception[68] and mandates the need for the virtue of discretion. More importantly, spiritual direction is needed to help develop and focus discernment. For Cassian, the soul which develops in charity becomes more and not less conscious of sin, for "even saints, and, if we may say, men who see, whose aim is the utmost perfection, cleverly detect in themselves even those things which the gaze of our mind being as it were darkened cannot see."[69] According to Cassian, the growing awareness of sin necessitated, especially for those who were thirsting for instruction in perfection, the need to grow in the process of discernment.[70]

Cassian sees that "there are plenty of roads to God,"[71] so that any man or woman had a chance for perfection; in the mood of the 4th century with its deep social divisions, it was easy to go astray in the sense of depriving ordinary men and women of any chance of perfection. The observation of rules or outward acts was important for

---

[64] *Ibid.* 10:12.
[65] Lk. 23:46; Ps. 31:5.
[66] *Inst.* 12:27.
[67] *Conf.* 6:14.
[68] Cf. *Conf.* 2:5, 7, 8.
[69] *Conf.* 23:6, 16.
[70] *Inst.* 12:29.
[71] *Conf.* 14:6.

Cassian, but what really mattered was what happened inwardly, the "state" of the soul; the practical and theoretical aspects of the inward journey were inextricably mingled. Cassian recognized that for growth in the spiritual life, especially for growth in prayer, there had to exist openness to the Holy Spirit and at least a desire for moral growth; one had to be receptive to the Word of God and this receptivity included the desire for growth in openness of heart.[72] This openness of heart allows for the humble and patient magnanimity of spiritual friendship for those actions guided by the Spirit.[73]

The openness of heart, which Cassian highlights as the ideal and describes in *Conf.* 12:8, includes obedience to discernment, when one has arrived at a spiritually confident self-control:

> He has without a doubt arrived at the state where he is the same at night as during the day; the same in reading as at prayer; the same alone as when surrounded by crowds of people; so that, finally, he never sees himself in secret as he would blush to be seen by men, and that inescapable eye does not see anything in him that he would wish to be hidden from human gaze.

The seeker sifts out and discerns clarity of moods and feelings from interior inspiration, but more often the person finds it through a spiritual guide who has found the "royal road" and whose purity of heart allows him to see, feel, or taste the will of God. Cassian, like Ignatius of Loyola and other spiritual authors, understands the need for realism and openness with one's spiritual guide. Otherwise, one will only be victimized and unable through God's grace in prayer to become more Christlike.

---

[72] Cf. *Inst.* 12:27.
[73] Cf. *Inst.* 9:11; *Conf.* 23:20; Gal. 5:24.

CHAPTER 5

CASSIAN AND
IGNATIUS OF LOYOLA

Among the many books which contributed to the early monastic roots of the spirituality of Ignatius of Loyola (1491–1556) are the *Flos Sanctorum* and the *Imitation of Christ*. The *Flos Sanctorum* (often called the *Golden Legend*)[1] was written by the Italian Dominican Jacobus de Voragine (1229–1298), Archbishop of Genoa, with literal excerpts from some of the early Christian sources such as Macarius, Antony, Basil, and Benedict.[2] Years later, while speaking of his conversion, Ignatius mentioned how impressed he was with the *Golden Legend*'s saintly models, especially St. Francis, St. Dominic, and St. Humphrey. The Egyptian desert saint, Onuphrius or Humphrey, who according to legend spent seventy years alone in the desert, became indelibly stamped on the memory of Ignatius.[3] Similarly, the *Imitation of Christ* by Thomas à Kempis provided Ignatius with an assortment of details mentioned by Cassian and other early monastic writers.[4]

Anyone familiar with the *Spiritual Exercises* of Ignatius of Loyola cannot help but see similarities between John Cassian and Ignatius, especially in the journey of prayer. Whether it is the value of patience,

---

[1] *The Golden Legend of Jacobus de Voragine*. Trans. and adapted from the Latin by Granger Ryan & Helmut Ripperger. Longmans, Green & Co., New York, 1941.

[2] See *Ignatius of Loyola, His Personality and Spiritual Heritage, 1556–1956*. Ed. by Friedrich Wulf, S.J., The Institute of Jesuit Sources, St. Louis, 1977; in particular, Study 7 entitled *"Early Monastic Elements in Ignatian Spirituality: Toward Clarifying Some Fundamental Concepts of the Exercises"* by Heinrich Bacht, S.J., pp. 200–236.

[3] James Brodrick, S.J., *Saint Ignatius Loyola. The Pilgrim Years*. London, Burns & Oates, 1956, p. 70; see also "El influjo de San Onofre in San Ignacio a base de un texto inédito de Nadal" by Pedro de Leturia. *Manresa* II (1926), 224–238, where Nadal mentions Humphrey (Ignatius does not cite his name) as one of the three saintly influences in the life of Ignatius.

[4] Cf. Book I, Ch. 18 and Book III, Ch. 54.

the dynamic of inner "struggle," the need for discretion and spiritual direction, the importance of imagery-imagination-memory, or the spiritual life characterized by indecision (or half measures [or inner freedom]), the Ignatian journey in prayer is intertwined with that of Cassian.

In the journey of prayer Cassian takes great pains to emphasize the need for preparation *before* the formal time of prayer[5] in order to deal with distractions and the instability of the human mind. As Germanus says:[6]

> the mind is constantly whirling from psalm to psalm, leaping from a gospel text to a reading from the Apostle, wandering from this to the prophesies and thence being carried away to certain spiritual histories, tossed about fickle and aimless through the whole body of Scripture. It is unable to reject or retain anything by its own doing, nor can it come to a conclusion about anything by fully judging or examining it, having become a mere *toucher and taster of spiritual meanings* and not a begetter and possessor of them.

Similarly, Ignatius uses the "additional directions"[7] and "preludes"[8] of the *Spiritual Exercises* to focus the mind, body, and soul before prayer in order to minimize distractions.

Once the time of prayer has begun, the virtues of humility and patience take priority for Cassian; this is especially true in any society inundated with the drive toward immediate gratification.[9] While Cassian sees patience as helping to diffuse the passion of anger, which is seen as destructive to growth in prayer,[10] Ignatius appreciates the value of patience related to prayer in his *Spiritual Exercises*, especially when considering the Rules for the Discernment of Spirits,[11] and in particular the state of desolation.[12] Nevertheless, according to Abba Piamun:[13]

---

[5] Cf. *Conf.* 10:14; see footnote #44 in Chapter 1.

[6] *Ibid.* 10:13.1; emphasis mine.

[7] *Sp. Ex.* 73, 74, etc.

[8] *Ibid.* 102–104, etc.

[9] See part 1 in Chapter 2.

[10] See footnote #57 in Chapter 1, 10 and 29 in Chapter 2.

[11] *Sp. Ex.* 313–336.

[12] *Ibid.* 321.

[13] *Conf.* 18:13.1.

patience would not be praiseworthy or admirable if it maintained its intended tranquillity without having been assailed by any of the enemy's darts, but it is distinguished and glorious when it remains unmoved while storms of trial break upon it.

It is the virtue of patience under attack, especially in trials during moments of weakness, that Cassian and Ignatius express the same experience of inner struggle. For Cassian, when

someone who has suffered mistreatment is inflamed with the fire of anger, it must not be believed that his bitterness at the abuse inflicted on him is the cause of his sin, but rather that it is the manifestation of *a hidden weakness.* This is in accordance with the parable of the Lord, the Savior, when he told about the two houses—one that was established on solid rock and the other on sand, upon the both of which there fell, he says, rainstorms and torrents and tempests. But the one that was established on solid rock experienced no damage from that violent onslaught, whereas the one that was built on the uncertain and shifting sands collapsed at once.[14] It appears to have caved in not, indeed, because it was struck by an outpouring of torrential rain but because it was foolishly built on sand.[15]

Ignatius, as Špidlík points out,[16] uses the following metaphor to express the same idea of vulnerability at a weak point:

the conduct of our enemy may also be compared to the tactics of a leader intent upon seizing and plundering a position he desires. A commander and leader of an army will encamp, explore the fortifications and defenses of the stronghold, and *attack at the weakest point.* In the same way, the enemy of our human nature investigates from every side all our virtues—theological, cardinal, and moral. Where he finds the defenses of eternal salvation weakest and most deficient, there he attacks and tries to take us by storm.[17]

---

[14] Cf. Mt. 7:24–27.

[15] *Conf.* 18:3; emphasis mine.

[16] *Ignazio di Loyola e la spiritualita orientale. Guida alla Lettura degli Esercizi* by Tomáš Špidlík, Edizioni Studium, Roma, 1994, p. 78.

[17] *Sp. Ex.* 327; emphasis mine.

The dynamic of inner "wrestling" or "struggle"[18] is important for Cassian during the journey in prayer; he highlights the fact that we "wrestle against"[19] demons in this inner journey.[20] Cassian[21] follows Evagrius[22] in developing a strategy for fighting various temptations and passions, and the essence of this strategy is manifest in the *Spiritual Exercises* of Ignatius.[23] This sense of "struggle" is utilized by Ignatius in his *Exercises* from Ephesians;[24] as Buckley says, "the struggle ranges immediately within the finite, between the human and the diabolical . . . the diabolical is the antihuman, the humanly destructive."[25] For the Fathers of the Desert, the soul matured only through discernment of spirits in battle.[26] Whether it is Origen,[27] Athanasius,[28] Evagrius,[29] or Cassian, the importance of discernment of spirits is obvious in the development of monastic spirituality and in the Ignatian view of discernment. While he follows this directive and insists on the need to secure "a power of discerning with unerring judgment the spirits" that rise up within oneself,[30] Cassian warns about giving higher forms of spiritual knowledge to the inexperienced.[31] Similarly, in the *Exercises*, Ignatius warns against giving the Rules for Discernment of the Second Week to someone who is "a person unskilled in spiritual things and is tempted grossly and openly, for example, by bringing before his mind obstacles to

---

[18] Cf. Eph. 6:12—"For it is not against human enemies that we have to struggle, but against the Sovereignties and the Powers who originate the darkness in this world, the spiritual army of evil in the heavens."

[19] Cf. *Inst.* 5:18; *Conf.* 7:21.

[20] See footnote #55 in Chapter 2.

[21] See part 2 in Chapter 2.

[22] Cf. Evagrius, *De mal. cog.*, PG 79: 1200D–1233A.

[23] Cf. *Sp. Ex.* 6–13, 32–37, 74, 142, 313–336, 345–351. Note "*Le discernement des esprits dans les Exercices spirituels de S. Ignace de Loyola*" by J. Clémence in RAM 17 (1951), 347–375, and RAM 18 (1952), 64–81.

[24] Cf. "*Ecclesial Mysticism in the Spiritual Exercises of Ignatius*" by Michael J. Buckley, S.J., TS 56 (1995), 441–463.

[25] *Ibid.*, p. 445.

[26] See footnote #81 in Chapter 3.

[27] Origen, *On Prayer*; see Hans Urs von Balthasar, *Origenes*, pp. 330–341.

[28] Athanasius, *Vita Antonii*; see Louis Bouyer, *Vie de Saint Antoine*, pp. 67–98, 142–144.

[29] See: Origen, *On Prayer* and Evagrius, *Chapters on Prayer* and *Praktikos*.

[30] *Conf.* 2:1; see footnote 26 in Chapter 3.

[31] *Ibid.*, 14:9, 17.

his advance in the service of God our Lord."[32] While Cassian prioritizes the importance of *discretio before* and during an inner struggle, an important element for Ignatius is the tactic of *counterattack*, of concentrating one's personal resources to rout the enemy by a courageous offense externalized in action *after* the soul has experienced inner movements.[33]

But, without the presence of discretion and spiritual direction, this inner "struggle" is like walking in a minefield. Ignatius uses Cassian's *Second Conference* of Abbot Moses in his letters to illustrate, as W. Young rightly confirms, that "the danger in the spiritual life is greater when one advances rapidly in it without the bridle of discretion,"[34] for, as Abbot Moses says, "by no other vice does the devil draw a monk headlong and bring him to death sooner than by persuading him to neglect the counsel of the elders and to trust his own judgment and decision."[35] As Bouyer indicates,[36] the spirituality of Ignatius is rooted in his appreciation of the Desert Fathers and early monasticism. Certainly this is true of the Ignatian view of obedience and the importance of discernment,[37] as merely a cursory reading of *Practice of Perfection and Christian Virtues*[38] by the Jesuit Alphonsus Rodríguez indicates. As Waddell says so eloquently about the Desert Fathers:

> And yet one intellectual concept they did give to Europe: eternity. Here again they do not formulate it: they embody it. These men, by the very exaggeration of their lives, stamped infinity on the imagination of the West.[39]

Cassian understands discretion as strengthening prayer, for "it is clearly shown that no virtue can possibly be perfectly acquired or continue without the grace of discretion."[40] Nevertheless, it is spiritual direction

---

[32] *Sp. Ex.* 9.

[33] *Ibid.*, 325.

[34] See *Letters of St. Ignatius of Loyola*, selected and translated by William J. Young, S.J., Loyola University Press, 1959, pp. 169, 291.

[35] *Conf.* 2:2.

[36] Louis Bouyer, *Du Protestantisme à l'Église*, Paris, 1954, p. 122.

[37] Cf. Hugo Rahner, "*Ignatius und die aszetische Tradition.*" ZAM 17 (1942), 66–72.

[38] First edition in 1609; first English translation in 1612.

[39] *The Desert Fathers* by Helen Waddell, p. 23.

[40] *Conf.* 2:4; see footnote 78 in Chapter 2.

which nurtures the discernment process[41] as well as growth in humility and spiritual self-knowledge.

During the journey in prayer, especially in any inner struggle, the devil often takes on the appearance of an "angel of light"[42] for Cassian. This use of "angel of light" imagery is reminiscent of the *Spiritual Exercises*[43] where Ignatius remarks that "it is a mark of the evil spirit to assume the appearance of an angel of light. He begins by suggesting thoughts that are suited to a devout soul, and ends by suggesting his own." While in general Greek authors saw pure prayer as free from imagery,[44] Syriac authors were more willing to utilize the role of memory and imagination (especially in the recollection of God and Holy Scripture) to help the wandering mind focus and discern fantasies in the gradual spiritual transformation which helped to establish a prayerful disposition.[45] While Evagrius warned that the memory must be controlled when we seek to pray for this, it is very difficult to pray while being affected by bad memories,[46] Cassian understood the utilization of memory along with the Holy Scripture[47] as an important means to attain a sense of unity in prayer, where the mind and heart are concentrated upon God; in fact, the memory of Holy Scripture for Cassian offered the possibility to stabilize an order and succession in *praxis*.[48] The similarity between the Ignatian conception of "a representation of the place by seeing it in imagination," an interior image,[49] and the Eastern Christian view of sacred images is striking; the point of connection is prayer.[50] In this context, it is useful to remember

---

[41] See footnote #67 in Chapter 3; cf. *Inst.* 4:9.

[42] 2 Cor. 11:14, *Conf.* 16:11. See *Conf.* 10:10, 9:34, 9:6, 10:11 and footnotes 63–64 in Chapter 2.

[43] *Sp. Ex.* 332; see footnote 13 in Chapter 3.

[44] Cf. *The Orthodox Church* by S. Bulgakov, London, 1935.

[45] Cf. *The Syriac Fathers on Prayer and the Spiritual Life*, intro. and trans. by Sebastian Brock, CSS 101 (1987); see, for example, Isaac of Nineveh (pp. 293–297). Also, *The Ascetical Homilies of Saint Isaac the Syrian*, trans. by the Holy Transfiguration Monastery, Boston, Mass., 1984, see homilies 1–6, 12, 21, 34, 36–37, 39–40, 48, 51, 54, 63, 66, and 74.

[46] Cf. *Chapters on Prayer*, 22, 44–46.

[47] Cf. *Conf.* 1:17, 14:10.

[48] See footnote 126 in Chapter 3.

[49] Cf. *Sp. Ex.* 235.

[50] Cf. Pavel Florensky, *Le porte regali. Saggio sull'icona*, Milano, 1977, pp. 58–74.

what P. Florensky writes on the *internal process* that gives birth to an icon:[51] the process from spiritual "vision" (in the mind of the artist) to real concrete form is mediated through prayer.

Finally, as mentioned earlier,[52] the cyclic quality of Cassian's prayer is prompted by a three-pronged movement, which is analogous to a "shopper-buyer-owner" mentality and characterized by indecision, half measures, and inner freedom, respectively. Ignatius presents a similar mentality with his "three classes of men";[53] we encounter a "wishbone-jawbone-backbone" mentality in the *Exercises* as illustrated in Lk. 14:7–24 (choosing places at table), Lk. 18:18–27 (the rich aristocrat), and Lk. 19:1–10 (Zacchaeus). Progress in the spiritual life for Ignatius as well as Cassian is somehow correlated with one's willingness to let go, with inner freedom, for where there is no risk, no challenge, there is no spiritual growth. Nevertheless, the *Exercises* of Ignatius, like the journey in prayer for Cassian, is no school of the will or an exclusive active/ascetical function. Both are characterized by a passive function which is produced by the Holy Spirit. It is this passive element with an emphasis on patience which Ignatius owes primarily to the early monastic writers, Cassian in particular.

AN IGNATIAN CONTEMPLATIVE IN ACTION

For this author, one of the most recent and personal examples of Ignatian spirituality and many of Cassian's characteristics for a spiritual journey grounded in discernment and prayer was the Rev. Walter J. Ciszek, S.J. With a deep appreciation for perseverance in prayer and the Lord's Prayer as his model, Walter developed a discerning soul. This small, stocky Polish Jesuit returned to the United States in 1963 from twenty-three years in Russian confinement. It had taken him fifty-nine years, five of those in solitary confinement in Moscow's dreaded Lubianka prison, to realize that progress in the spiritual life was correlated with one's willingness to let go, with inner freedom, for where there was no risk, no challenge, there was no spiritual growth.

---

[51] *Ibid.* p. 74.

[52] See part 1 in Chapter 4.

[53] *Sp. Ex.* 149–157.

PURIFICATION: FROM TOTAL BLACKNESS TO BLINDING LIGHT

As with any spiritual journey concerned with growth in prayer, there is always a purification process. The "sinking feeling of helplessness and powerlessness" overcame Walter after his arrest in Russia in 1941 when he lost total control of his life.[54] He felt "completely cut off from everything and everyone who might conceivably help" him.[55] Considered a Vatican spy, he was transferred to Lubianka prison where men where reportedly "broken in body and spirit."[56] As he had done in every crisis in the past when there was no one to turn to, Walter "turned to God in prayer."[57]

While an interior voice helped him focus his faith, it was faith in prayer that sustained Walter, was his principle of life and always made him God-conscious. It was the same faith that made him conscious of his readiness and natural competency to handle whatever came along. Although he was persistent, many people characterized it as stubbornness. He "was naturally stubborn and strong-willed". . . having spent a great part of his life "developing willpower and training the will."[58] The tension between persistence and stubbornness, developed early in his life, gradually helped him become aware of God's patience and his need to become a patient pupil. Because he realized early that self-control was not enough in struggling against depression, fear, and insecurity, spiritual growth was contingent on the depth of his personal relationship with God. After his arrest, the measure of this depth was gauged almost exclusively by the quality of his prayer life which had been finely honed from an early age by ascetical practices.

Walter's asceticism in Lubianka became a life of prayer and humble faith in God. It was in prayer that self-conversion started and never ended. The absolute silence of God during solitary confinement suggested that he give in to his interrogators. Instead, he turned to prayer and persevered in it until the suggestion vanished. Persevering in prayer countered loneliness, confusion, and worthlessness, and led to continuous prayer; suffering patiently the internal dilemma of per-

---

[54] He leadeth Me (HLM) by Walter J. Ciszek, S.J., with Daniel Flaherty, S.J., Doubleday & Co., Inc., New York, 1973, p. 45.

[55] Ibid., p. 45.

[56] Ibid., p. 53.

[57] Ibid., p. 48.

[58] Ibid., p. 58.

severing in prayer was the prerequisite for finding that loneliness was the grace of faith given at that moment. He sensed deeply the frustrating pains of loneliness, confusion, and worthlessness, while at the same time, accepted all these in the spirit of faith and continued to serve God without change or compromise. The light of grace disclosed sufficiently to his mind the need of personal purification. Faith showed that this purification was an interior process manifest in humbly begging God's mercy, trustful fear of Him, and a readiness to do whatever the divine will proposed at any time. And there was a lot of time.

For some in Lubianka the time passed quickly, while for others, the seconds passed like minutes and even hours. There was only one constant in Lubianka—the "total and all-pervading silence that seemed to close-in around [him] and threaten [him] constantly,"[59] while "the agonizing afterthoughts that filled the hours in [his] silent cell after each period of interrogation . . . began to have their effect and eat away at [his] morale. It was then, especially, that [he] turned to prayer."[60] While "Lubianka, in many ways, was a school of prayer" for him,[61] it was a "tempering and purifying" experience for his soul.[62] During his first year in Lubianka, Walter "underwent a purging" of self that left him "cleansed to the bone."[63] The mental blackness in which he found himself allowed him no options but fear of self.[64] In this inner darkness he experienced despair, lost hope and sight of God, and even for a moment lost the last shreds of his faith in God.[65] Nevertheless, instinctively he turned to prayer and almost immediately was consoled by our Lord's agony in the garden. He had gone from "total blackness" to "an experience of blinding light" in what he could only call "a conversion experience" that changed his life.[66] From that moment he knew exactly what he must do and completely abandoned himself into God's hands[67] with a readiness to let Christ fully transform him.

---

[59] Ibid., p. 55.

[60] Ibid., p. 58.

[61] Ibid., p. 65.

[62] Ibid., p. 78.

[63] Ibid., p. 77.

[64] Ibid., p. 82.

[65] Ibid.

[66] Ibid., pp. 82–83.

[67] Ibid., p. 83.

While the shock of Lubianka left him horrified, instinctively he turned to God after he failed to do it alone and began to live the psalmist's words: "my days are in Thy hands."[68] There was never too little time for he knew that it was not he but God alone who had given him the exact time needed to work out his salvation. He could say that "in moments of human discouragement, the consciousness that [I] was fulfilling God's will in all that happened to [me] would serve to dispel all doubt and desolation."[69] In the silence of his cell, Walter began to realize that it was not self-will or willpower that mattered in the spiritual realm. Rather, it was the consciousness of God's grace working within and demanding full conformity of all his natural powers in whatever way grace was given in concrete circumstances; the interrogations had convinced him of that.

DISCERNMENT: A SEEING SOUL

The interrogators of Lubianka could be both kind and deceptive. Walter knew that often the devil took on the appearance of an angel of light while manifesting the ultimate in deceit and confusion, especially in the inner struggle during the journey in prayer. Interior moods, feelings, and movements had to be sifted out, discerned, so that he could recognize the Lord's call at the intimate core of his being. Because he knew that in the absence of the recollection of God, temptation would not be far behind; discernment became the eye and lamp of his body.[70]

The last four years in Lubianka allowed our Lord to continue fine-tuning Walter's soul. If anything, Lubianka gave him the spirit of prayer, courage, trust in God, and a deep appreciation of grace, even when he seemed worthless. All things considered, he realized that it was a question of ordering his life according to the truths found in the Lord's Prayer and he understood these as being summed-up by the one principal truth of doing the will of God the Father. As was the case with earlier spiritual writers, Walter viewed this prayer as a model given to us by Christ. It provided the essence of his definition of prayer: an invitation to lift the mind and heart to God the Father with a concern not only for the words of the prayer, but also for an appreciation of the mode of silence in which our Lord prayed and he now experienced. It

---

[68] Cf. Ps. 30:16.

[69] HLM, p. 172.

[70] Cf. Mt. 6:22–23.

was the perfect example of the Christian prayer of petition and contained the fullness of perfection. As the result of a direct privilege of grace and enlightened discretion, Walter immediately realized the full effect of his Lubianka conversion. He now had a single vision of Christ in all things, and the desire *to discern* His will in every situation.

He had to rise "from the tomb of Lubianka"[71] before our Lord could use him and before he could really appreciate His words: "Behold I send you as sheep in the midst of wolves."[72] Lubianka was in many ways like his Jesuit novitiate experience where he was "alone with God as it were on the mountaintop"[73] and able to develop the habit of recollection. Nevertheless, the prison experience had not prepared him for life after forced silence. Although he had a propensity to a life of prayer from early childhood, Walter's habit of recollection broke down after his release from Lubianka. He was "continuously distracted" by the "rough and ready realities of life,"[74] especially on prison trains heading for labor camps with hardcore criminals who thought nothing of killing at the slightest provocation.[75] Indeed, he came to appreciate the scriptural text "the children of this world are more astute in dealing with their own kind than are the children of light."[76] The first thing Walter discovered after release from Lubianka was "the presence of evil."[77] He came face-to-face with the criminal world and "for the first time . . .palpably experienced the power of evil and how completely it could overshadow the power of good."[78]

Motivation to restrain himself from doing evil or to abandon evil practices, already acquired during early years, came not from reason but from his conscience. This interior and mysterious voice demanded correction and yet his struggle with conscience lasted for years. Still, it was by means of the freedom to discern between good and evil, that Walter was able to make a progressive return to his full, original freedom: The spiritual freedom which required "an attitude of acceptance and openness to the will of God, rather than some planned

---

[71] HLM, p. 89.
[72] Cf. Mt. 10:16.
[73] HLM, p. 90.
[74] Ibid.
[75] Ibid., p. 91.
[76] Cf. Lk. 16:8.
[77] HLM., p. 90.
[78] Ibid., p. 91.

approach or calculated method."[79] While he "was still a prisoner" after his release from Lubianka, he nevertheless "felt free and liberated."[80] There was no anger or bitterness but peace and a deep sense of internal freedom. The forced Lubianka silence was gone and with it the easy prayerful recollection. The need to *listen* for the interior voice of conscience and *discern* God's will in every situation became critical if he was to enter into a relationship with the living Lord. The concentration and attention required in prayer were not acts that deprived him of true freedom, but simply steps leading him to a gradual fuller freedom in God. He knew that there was no virtue without freedom, for as St. Paul said "The Lord is the Spirit, but where the Spirit of the Lord is there is liberty."[81] Walter could testify from his own experiences, especially from his darkest hours in Lubianka, "that the greatest sense of freedom along with peace of soul and abiding sense of security, comes when man totally abandons his own will in order to follow the will of God."[82]

Accepting such an attitude, his soul learned "to act not on its own initiative, but in response to whatever demands were imposed by God in the concrete instances of each day."[83] He experienced the need to sift the inner movements of his soul and respond to the constant question: Was the Lord revealing Himself, and if so, what was He saying? The basic discernment between good and evil required that he grow in inner awareness and the ability to see clearly into himself. While he knew discernment had for its goal to discover who was Jesus and where His reign was found, Walter tested every spirit to see if it came from God. He had begun to develop a seeing soul. His spiritual growth now was intimately connected with the examination of anything that entered his heart to see if and how he should respond. With St. Paul he could say "every thought is our prisoner, captured to be brought into obedience to Christ."[84]

Most of us can identify with at least a modified form of the feelings of helplessness, powerlessness, and despair experienced by Walter in the silence of Lubianka. By abandoning himself to God's will, his

---

[79] Ibid., p. 173.

[80] Ibid., p. 89.

[81] Cf. 2 Cor. 3:17.

[82] HLM, pp. 171–172.

[83] Ibid., p. 173.

[84] Cf. 2 Cor. 10:5.

journey in prayer echoed the spiritual journeys of many saints in the past. And yet, there was an uniqueness in Walter's journey, and certainly in his cross, that made him a model for many Christians today, especially in these troubled times. The conversion experience in a silent cell left him with an unconditional readiness to change his life and place everything in God's hands. Lubianka provided the nails for his cross and the necessary purification for a saintly life of priestly service grounded in discernment and prayer.

CONCLUSION

Personal and intelligent evil moves cunningly along the lines of contemporary fads and interests, and within the usual bounds of the experience of ordinary men and women. There is little room for moral ambiguity. All life seems to be a struggle between positive and negative impulses and the choices all of us make every day whether to pursue our loftiest goals or to give up. Whether one is tempted to believe that there exists no difference between good and evil, where all values are subject only to one's personal preferences, or that there can be no relevance for the modern person in anything that cannot be rationally understood, moral value is confused with absence of any value. There exists an inner voice, barely audible at first but then lashing out at the attempted entry of any singular beauty or grace. Evil's prime weapon of confusion has found a home where, as Abbot Joseph says, "'Satan transforms himself into an angel of light' (2 Cor. 11:14). In this way he fraudulently pours a dark and foul obscurity over our thoughts in place of the true light of knowledge."[1] Cassian utilizes growth in prayer to diffuse this weapon.

According to Abbot Isaac, "every mind is upbuilt and formed in its prayer according to the degree of its purity."[2] Cassian understood anger as destructive to growth in purity of prayer,[3] and patience as helping to diffuse this passion. Whether a demon or the troubled subconscious, the result is the same: a temptation. Cassian presents a strikingly real picture of the operations of demons in their constant battle with people, and this battle intensifies as a person's interior life of perseverance in prayer develops. As prayer matures, discretion helps to moderate excesses and nurture growth of virtues. The enemy does its best to attack the virtues created by a growing interior disposition centered on prayer and a person's hard labor and perseverance during prayer.[4] Influenced by a well-developed tradition of the Desert Fathers in his treatment of temptations

---

[1] *Conf.* 16:11.
[2] *Ibid.*, 10:6.
[3] *Ibid.*, 9:3.
[4] *Ibid.*, 2:13, 7:6, 9:2.

and vulnerability to deception, Cassian understands that the inner struggle or wrestling with any form of deception provides a profitable opportunity for growth in prayer.

In any society immersed in a culture of excess, the temptation toward promiscuity and immediate self-gratification is always present. Cassian realizes the importance of managing these conditions if peace of heart is to be allowed to tend toward continual and unbroken perseverance in prayer. He understands progress in the spiritual life as directly linked to growth in prayer, which is nurtured by patient self-control, discretion, and charity. For Cassian, discretion and spiritual direction were means to help in the purgation of what was evil while prayer nurtured the cultivation of what was good. Whether purgation or cultivation, the change or "becoming" was dynamic and at a new level of virtue. For him, this dynamic change is intimately connected with discretion and spiritual direction, two effects of growth in prayer.

In many of the cases related by Cassian there exist stories concerning deceived holy men of the desert. Whether it was a case of being "deluded by the cleverness of demons,"[5] "welcoming a demon in the guise of angelic brightness,"[6] or being "deceived by diabolical revelations and dreams,"[7] the one deceived possessed little of the virtue of discretion. Often the devil takes on the appearance of an angel of light while manifesting the ultimate in deceit and confusion, especially in the inner struggle during the journey in prayer where, as Abbot Isaac says, "our prayers should be insistent and without the hesitation born of lack of confidence";[8] one only unmasks him by the *discretio* in the works, in controlling the excessiveness, confusion, and lack of equilibrium toward which he pushes us. Later, Ignatius of Loyola would remark in his *Spiritual Exercises*[9] that "it is a mark of the evil spirit to assume the appearance of an angel of light. He begins by suggesting thoughts that are suited to a devout soul, and ends by suggesting his own." While the suggestions,[10] at times, can be strong enough to cause interventions of hesitation, confusion, and despair in our prayer, the

---

[5] *Ibid.*, 2:5.
[6] *Ibid.*, 2:7.
[7] *Ibid.*, 2:8.
[8] *Ibid.*, 9:34.
[9] Cf. *Sp. Ex.* 332.
[10] Cf. *Conf.* 10:10–11.

interventions can result in a breakdown of confidence in otherwise prayerful petition. Cassian understands that

> this confusion certainly besets us because we do not keep something special fixed before our eyes as a kind of formula to which the errant mind can be recalled after numerous detours and divagations and into which it can enter, as into a safe harbor, after repeated shipwrecks.[11]

While confusion in most instances is caused by an inability to control distractions and focus the mind and heart, vulnerability to any onslaught of evil is normally greater once a disposition of peace and high virtue has been achieved in the journey of prayer. Self-control, especially concerning thoughts, plays a key part in any life of prayer, for Cassian and he even suggest that one's "whole attention should thus be fixed on one point, and the rise and circle of all his thoughts be vigorously restricted to it."[12] Cassian highlights the importance of focusing prayer through brevity, frequency, and repetition in order to nurture the internal disposition for incessant prayer, because he understands constant prayer in the heart as helping to develop "an impregnable wall for all who are laboring under the attacks of demons."[13] Growth in incessant prayer allows the spiritual journey to be guided and focused toward an internal absorption, where our Lord brings the soul back within the "eyes of the heart"[14] and the soul sees itself illuminated by celestial light. It is this inward illumination, regardless of how small at first, which provides nutrition for spiritual self-confidence.

The spiritual journey involves continual recollection of God and incessant prayer where growth in the virtues, especially humility and patience, nurtures growth in faith-filled confidence: not fleeting and worldly confidence but that which is rooted, nurtured, and sustained by our Lord's presence. One no longer depends on externals but now relies on a God-centered internal disposition, the "inner man."[15] Nevertheless, faith-filled confidence in prayer is always tempered for Cassian by hu-

---

[11] *Ibid.*, 10:8.
[12] *Ibid.*, 24:6.
[13] *Ibid.*, 10:10.
[14] *Ibid.*, 10:6; see also *Inst.* 5:34 and *Conf.* 1:13, 3:7, 14:9, 23:6.
[15] *Conf.* 18:16.

mility and purity of conscience[16] and leads to an inner freedom of openness in the spiritual life.[17]

Cassian has a practical and optimistic view of the spiritual life wherein prayer continually nurtures the growth process in perfection. Regardless of the level of one's prayer life, each person may offer up pure and devout prayers as a consequence of the heart being touched by contrition. The concomitant result of each divine touch is the potential for gradual growth in the "state" of prayer. Cassian understands prayer as a "state" which, as I. Hausherr admits, "shares the characteristics of habit or disposition."[18] The practice of prayer is nourished by memory filled with Scripture and good thoughts and is conditioned gradually to arrive at continual recollection of God in order to develop a God-centered internal disposition. One becomes not only a toucher or taster but also an owner of spiritual meanings. The inward recollection of God manifests itself on the outside by prayer being made one's own only to be fulfilled in one's daily life. Like Benedict, who models his Rule on many of Cassian's practical aspects, Ignatius of Loyola utilizes Cassian's journey of prayer to enrich one's journey through his *Spiritual Exercises,* where progress in the spiritual life is somehow correlated with a mentality of inner freedom—an internal freedom in God as found by Walter Ciszek.

The "shopper-buyer-owner" mentality, characterized by indecision, half measures, and inner freedom, respectively, is a spiritual journey whereon most people have problems, especially those who are result-oriented. Most individuals find it difficult at best to get beyond the "buyer" level, and if they do reach the "owner" level there is the persistent problem of remaining at that level or returning there with some regularity. Cassian is a realist and appreciates this problem. He is extremely practical and knows the importance of adapting ascetical practices to culture and state of life. He highlights the importance of the internal disposition created and nurtured by prayer and its relationship

---

[16] *Ibid.,* 9:32–33.

[17] *Ibid.,* 10:12.

[18] NJH, pp. 138–139. Cassian views the "Our Father" as a model for prayer given to us by Christ. As S. Marsili says (see Marsili, *op. cit.,* p. 55), it is this model which Cassian wants to use to teach a "state" of prayer; a state that is not only concerned with the words of the prayer but beyond this is striving for an appreciation of the mode of silence (see part 2 in Chapter 1) in which our Lord prayed. For Cassian, the Our Father "contains the fullness of perfection" (*Conf.* 9:25).

with discretion and self-control. It is an internal disposition focused on incessant prayer which encourages a steadfastness of heart.

Part of each spiritual journey in prayer for John Cassian is the inner struggle between one's sensitivity to God's voice within and a self-preoccupied state of solitude. The state of solitude can engender within itself an indifference to evil, the beginning of the loss of shame, and eventually a distaste for good, while openness of heart lends itself to appreciate the importance of repentance in the long and hard process of stripping away any built-in insulation which inhibits growth in prayer.

For Cassian, prayer involves a process of growth which is conditioned "little by little"—from the state of the soul before prayer to the soul's condition during prayer. In any journey of prayer a state may eventually be reached where words are not necessary. Internal union with God through pure prayer can take the form of silence; it is prayer without words. In general, Cassian is ascetically practical and carries on the Alexandrian tradition of Origen and Evagrius.[19] He tries to set forth methodically the way in which prayer should be practiced if one is to attain its highest regions, especially the spontaneous gift of the prayer of fire and the concomitant gift of tears. This is clearly true in the value he places on short prayer.

---

[19] Cf. Olphe-Galliard, "Cassien," DSAM 2: 224.

ABBREVIATIONS

ABR	American Benedictine Review
ACW	Ancient Christian Writers series. Westminister, Maryland, 1946–.
AGG	Abhandlung der Gesellschaft der Wissenschaften zu Göttingen. Göttingen, 1843–.
ANF	Ante-Nicene Fathers. Rpt. Grand Rapids, 1978.
CC	*Collectanea cisterciensia*
CE	*Coptic Encyclopedia*
CIS	*Centrum Ignatianum Spiritualitatis.* Rome, 1979–.
Conf.	Conferences
CS	*Cistercian Studies*
CSCO	*Corpus Scriptorum Christianorum Orientalium.* Louvain, 1903–.
CSEL	*Corpus Scriptorum Ecclesiasticorum Latinorum.* Vienna, 1866–.
CSS	Cistercian Studies Series. Spencer, Washington, Kalamazoo, 1969–.
DACL	*Dictionnaire d'Archéologie Chrétienne et de Liturgie.*
De Incarn.	*De Incarnatione Domini Contra Nestorium*
DESp	*Dizionario Enciclopedico di Spiritualita*, ed. Emmanuel Ancilla. Volumes 1–2, Rome, 1975.
De Vir. Ill.	*De Viris Illustribus*
DHGE	*Dictionnaire d'Histoire et de Géographie Ecclésiastique.* Paris, 1912–.
DIP	*Dizionario degli Istituti di Perfezione.* Rome, 1973–.
Dk	*Diakonia*
DP	*Dizionario Patristico e di Antichita Cristiane*
DSAM	*Dictionnaire de Spiritualité Ascétique et Mystique*
DTC	*Dictionnaire de Théologie Catholique.* Paris, 1903–1950.
ECQ	*The Eastern Churches Quarterly*
ECR	*Eastern Churches Review*
FZPT	*Freiburger Zeitschrift für Philosophie und Theologie*
GCS	Die griechischen christlichen Schriftsteller, Berlin-Leipzig, 1897–.
GL	*Geist und Leben*
Inst.	The Institutes
JEH	*Journal of Ecclesiastical History*
MS	*Monastic Studies*
NCE	New Catholic Encyclopedia
NJH	I. Hausherr, *The Name of Jesus.* CSS 44, Cistercian Pub., Kalamazoo, Mich., 1978.

NPNF	*A Select Library of the Nicene and Post-Nicene Fathers*. Rpt. Grand Rapids, 1979.
OC	*Orientalia Christiana*. Rome, 1923–1934.
OCA	*Orientalia Christiana Analecta*. Rome, 1935–.
OCP	*Orientalia Christiana Periodica*. Rome, 1935–.
PG	Jacobus Paulus Migne, *Patrologia Graeca* (Paris 1857–1866)
PL	Jacobus Paulus Migne, *Patrologia Latina* (Paris 1841–1864)
PO	*Patrologia Orientalis*. Paris, 1903–.
RAM	*Revue d'Ascétique et de Mystique*. Toulouse, 1920–.
RB	*Revue bénédictine*
REA	*Revue des études augustiniennes*
RHR	*Revue de l'Histoire des Religions*. Paris, 1880–.
RHS	Revue d'historie de la spiritualité
RR	*Review for Religious*
RSR	*Recherches de Science Religieuse*. Paris, 1910–.
RTAM	*Recherches de théologie ancienne et médiévale*
SA	*Studia Anselmiana*. Rome, 1933–.
SC	*Sources Chrétiennes*, Paris, 1941–.
SHI	T. Špidlík, *The Spirituality of the Christian East. A Systematic Handbook*. CSS 79, Cistercian Pub., Kalamazoo, Mich., 1986.
SHII	T. Špidlík, *La Spiritualité de l'Orient Chrétien. II. La Priere*, OCA 230, Rome, 1988.
SM	*Studia Monastica*
SP	*Studia Patristica*
Sp. Ex.	Spiritual Exercises of St. Ignatius of Loyola
SVTQ	*St. Vladimir's Theological Quarterly*
TRE	*Theologische Realenzyklopädie*
TS	*Theological Studies*
TU	Texte und Untersuchungen
VS	*La Vie Spirituelle*
WS	*Word & Spirit*
ZAM	*Zeitschrift für Aszese und Mystik*, Würzburg, 1926–.
ZKG	Zeitschrift für Kirchengeschichte
ZKTH	*Zeitschrift für katholische Theologie*, Wien, 1877–.

SELECT GLOSSARY

Acēdia	- sloth, weariness
Agapē	- love
Apatheia	- a "purity of heart" which allows one to see, feel, or taste the will of God
Askēsis	- spiritual training, work
Diakrisis	- basic discernment of good and evil
Discretion	- the charism of proper judgment which helps one avoid the sin of excess in any undertaking and teaches one always to walk along the "royal road"
Eight principal faults	- gluttony, fornication, avarice, melancholy, anger, *acēdia*, vainglory, pride
Exagoreusis	- manifestation of thoughts
Hēsychia	- quiet, stillness, tranquillity
Jesus Prayer	- Lord Jesus Christ, Son of God, have mercy on me a sinner
Kardia	- heart
Kardiakē proseuchē	- prayer of the heart
Katastasis	- condition, settled state
Katastatis tēs proseuchēs	- the state of prayer, an habitual disposition
Logismoi	- passionate thoughts, deadly sins
Nēpsis	- attention, vigilance, sobriety
Oratio ignita	- fiery prayer
Praktikē	- contemplation of the physical world, the ascetic life
Praxis	- act, action, deed
Proseuchē	- prayer
Prosochē	- attention
Theōria	- spiritual knowledge, contemplation, vision
Theōria physikē	- contemplation of nature
Theōsis	- deification

SELECT BIBLIOGRAPHY

Abel, Otto. *Studien zu dem gallischen Presbyter Johannes Cassianus.* Munich, Wolf, 1904.

Appel, Regis. *"Cassian's* Discretio: *A Timeless Virtue."* ABR 17 (1966), 20–29.

Bacht, Heinrich. *"'Meditatio' in den ältesten Mönchsquellen."* GL 28 (1955), 360–373.

Bagnall, Roger S. *Egypt in Late Antiquity.* Princeton, Princeton University Press, 1993.

Balthasar, Hans Urs von. "Die Hiera des Evagrius Pontikus," ZKTH 63, 1939.

_____. "Metaphysik und Mystik des Evagrius Ponticus," ZAM 14, 1939.

Bamberger, John Eudes (trans.). *Evagrius Ponticus: Praktikos and Chapters on Prayer*, CSS 4, Cistercian Pub., Kalamazoo, MI., 1981.

Bardy, Gustave. "Origene" in DTC, Tome XI. Paris: Librairie Letouzey et Ane, 1932, pp. 1489–1565.

_____. "Apatheia," DSAM 1 (1937), 727–734.

Bartelink, G.J.M. *Athanase d'Alexandrie: Vie d'Antoine.* SC 400 (1994).

Bauer, Franz. "Die Heilige Schrift bei den Mönchen des christlichen Altertums." *Theologie und Glaube* 17 (1925), 512–532.

Beggiani, Seely. *Introduction to Eastern Christian Spirituality: The Syriac Tradition*, University of Scranton Press, 1991.

Bonar, Clyde A. "Scripture Prayer Program on Compunction," RR, May–June 1989, pp. 387–393.

Bourguignon, P. & Wenner, F. "Combat spirituel," DSAM 2, 1 (1953), col. 1135–1142.

Bousset, Wilhelm. *Apophthegmata. Studien zur Geschichte des ältesten Mönchtums.* Tübingen, Mohr, 1923.

_____. "Das Mönchtum der sketischen Wüste." ZKG 42 (1926), 1–41.

Bouyer, Louis. *Du Protestantisme à l'Église*, Paris, 1954.

_____. *A History of Christian Spirituality*, 3 vols., New York: Desclee Co., 1960.

_____. *Introduction to Spirituality*, New York: Desclee Co., 1961.

Bradshaw, Paul. *Daily Prayer in the Early Church*, Alcuin Club Collections No. 63, London: SPCK 1981.

Brame, Grace A. "The Prayer of Jesus and Its Relationship to Hesychasm and Orthodox Spirituality" in *Patristic & Byzantine Review* 5, 1 (1986), 48–60.

Brand, Charles. *"Le De Incarnatione Domini de Jean Cassien."* Contribution a l'etude de la christologie en Occident a la veille du Concile d'Ephese. Doctoral diss., University of Strasbourg, 1954.

Bremond, Jean. *Les Peres du desert* (les Moralistes chretiens), Paris, 1927.

Brock, Sebastian. *The Syriac Fathers on Prayer and the Spiritual Life*, intro. & trans., CSS 101 (1987).

Brodrick, James. *Saint Ignatius Loyola. The Pilgrim Years*. London, Burns & Oates, 1956.

Brown, Peter. *The Body and Society. Men, Women and Sexual Renunciation in Early Christianity*. New York, Columbia University Press, 1988.

Buckley, Michael J. "*Ecclesial Mysticism in the Spiritual Exercises of Ignatius*." TS 56 (1995), 441–463.

Bulgakov, Sergius. *The Orthodox Church*. London, 1935.

Bunge, Gabriel. "Évagre le Pontique et les deux Macaire." *Irénikon* 56 (1983), 215–227, 323–360.

_____. *Evagrios Pontikos: Briefe aus der Wüste*. Sophia 24. Trier, Paulinus-Verlag, 1986.

_____. "Origenismus-Gnostizismus. Zum geistgeshichtlichen Standort des Evagrios Pontikos." *Vigiliae Christianae* 40 (1986), 24–54.

_____. *Das Geistgebet. Studien zum Traktat De oratione des Evagrios Ponti-kos*. Koln, Luthe-Verlag, 1987.

_____. "The 'Spiritual Prayer': On the Trinitarian Mysticism of Evagrius of Pontus." MS 17 (1987), 191–208.

_____. "'*Priez sans cesse': aux origines de la prière hésychaste*." SM 30 (1988) 7–16.

_____. *Geistliche Vaterschaft: Christliche Gnosis bei Evagrios Pontikos*, Regensburg, 1988.

_____. *Akedia. Die geistliche Lehre des Evagrios Pontikos vom Überdruss*, Cologne, 1989.

_____. *Evagrios Pontikos: Praktikos oder der Mönch, Hundert Kapitel uber das geistliche Leben*. Koln, Luthe-Verlag, 1989.

_____. "*Mysterium unitatis. Der Gedanke der Einheit von Schöpfer und Geschöpf in der evagrianischen Mystik*." FZPT 36 (1989), 449–469.

_____. "'*Der mystische Sinn der Schrift': Anlässlich der Veröffentlichung der Scholien zum Ecclesiasten des Evagrios Pontikos*." SM 36 (1994), 135–146.

Burke, E. M. "*Grace*" in NCE, Vol. 6. New York: McGraw-Hill Book Co., 1967, pp. 658–672.

Burton-Christie, Douglas. *The Word in the Desert: Scripture and the Quest for Holiness in Early Christian Monasticism*. New York, Oxford University Press, 1993.

Butler, Cuthbert. *Benedictine Monachism. Studies in Benedictine Life and Rule*. London, Longmans, Green & Co., 1919.

_____. *The Lausiac History of Palladius*. Vol. 1, *A Critical Discussion together with notes on Early Egyptian Monasticism*. Vol. 2, *The Greek Text Edited with Introduction and Notes*. Text and Studies 6. Cambridge, Cambridge University Press, 1898 and 1904.

_____. *Western Mysticism*, 2nd ed. London: Constable Publications, 1951.

Cabassut, Andre. "*Discretion*." DSAM 3: 1311–1330.

Cabrol, Fernand. *"Cassien."* DACL 2: 2348–2357.

Canévet, Mariette. *"Sens spirituels."* DSAM 14: 598–617.

Cappuyns, M. *"Cassien."* DHGE 11: 1319–1348.

Cassian, John. *De Incarnatione domini libri* VII (*De Incarn.*). Ed. Michael Petschenig. CSEL 17 (Vienna, 1888).

_____. *De institutis coenobiorum et de octo principalium vitiorum remediis libri* XII (*Inst.*) Ed. Michael Petschenig. CSEL 17 (Vienna, 1888).

_____. *Conlationes* XXIIII (*Conf.*). Ed. Michael Petschenig. CSEL 13 (Vienna, 1886).

Chadwick, Owen. *"Cassianus."* TRE 7: 650–657.

_____. *John Cassian. A Study in Primitive Monasticism.* Cambridge, Cambridge University Press, 1950, and 2nd ed., 1968.

Chitty, Derwas J. *The Desert a City: An Introduction to the Study of Egyptian and Palestinian Monasticism under the Christian Empire.* Oxford, Blackwell, 1966.

Ciszek, Walter J. with Daniel Flaherty. *He Leadeth Me.* Doubleday & Co., Inc., New York, 1973.

Clarkson, Benedict. *"The Rule of St. Benedict and the Concept of Self-Actualization."* CS 10, 1 (1975), 22–45.

Clémence, J. *"Le discernement des esprits dans les Exercices spirituels de S. Ignace de Loyola."* RAM 17 (1951), 347–375; also, RAM 18 (1952), 64–81.

Codina, Victor. *El aspecto cristologico en la espiritualidad de Juan Casiano.* OCA 175. Rome, 1966.

Colombás, García M. *San Benito su Vida y su Regla.* Madrid: Biblioteca de Autores Cristianos, 1954.

_____. *El Monacato Primitivo.* Vols. 1 & 2. Madrid: Biblioteca de Autores Cristianos, 1975.

_____. *La Tradicion Benedictina, Ensayo historico.* Vol.1, Zamora, 1989.

Coman, Jean. "Les 'Scythes' Jean Cassien et Denys le Petit." *Kleronomia* 7 (1975), 27–46.

Conio, C. "Theory and Practice in Evagrius Ponticus," in *Philosophy Theory and Practice, Proceedings of the International Seminar on World Philosophy,* edited by T.M.P. Mahadevan, Madras, 1974.

Corbishley, T. *"Mysticism."* NCE 10 (1967), 175–179.

Cristiani, Leon. *Jean Cassien. La spiritualite du desert.* Ed. De Fontenelle; Abbaye S. Wandrille, 1946.

Crouzel, Henri. *Origen.* trans. A.S. Worrall. San Francisco, Harper & Row, 1989.

_____. *Origène et la connaissance mystique.* Museum Lessianum section théologique 56. Toulouse, Desclée de Brouwer, 1961.

_____. "Origenism." *Sacramentum Mundi*, Vol.4. New York: Herder & Herder, 1969, pp. 327–328.

Cuper, Guillaume. "De Sancto Joanne Cassiano Abbate Massiliae in Gallia." In *Acta Sanctorum Iulii.* Vol. 5, pp. 458–482. Paris, Palmé, 1868.

Damian, Theodor. *"Some Critical Considerations and New Arguments Reviewing the Problem of St. John Cassian's Birthplace."* OCP 57 (1991), 257–280.

Davril, A. *"La Psalmodie chez les peres du desert,"* CC 49 (1987), 132–139.

Deferrari, Roy J. Théologie de l'image de Dieu chez Origene. *Théologie de la vie monastique.* Théologie 34 (1956), Paris.

_____. "Origene, precurseur du monachisme." *Théologie de la vie monastique.* Théologie 49 (1961), 15–38.

_____. "Recherches sur Origene et son influence," *Bulletin de Litterature Ecclesiastique* 62 (1961), 3–15, 105–113.

_____. "Origen and Origenism." NCE 10 (1967), 767–774.

De Goedt, M. *"L'extase dans la Bible."* DSAM 4: 2072–2087.

Dekkers, Eligius. "Les traductions grecques des écrits patristiques latins." *Sacris Eruditi* 5 (1953), 193–233.

Delatte, Paul. *Commentary on the Rule of St. Benedict.* Latrope, PA: The Archabbey Press, 1959.

Dembinska, M. "Diet: A Comparison of Food Consumption between some Eastern and Western Monasteries in the Fourth–Twelfth Centuries." *Byzantion* 55 (1985), 431–462.

Des Places, Edouard. *"Diadoque de Photicé."* DSAM 3: 817–834.

Devos, Paul. "Saint Jean Cassien et Saint Moïse l'Éthiopien." *Analecta Bollandiana* 103 (1985), 61–73.

Dingjan, Fr. "La discretion dans les apophtegmes des Peres," *Angelicum* 39 (1962), 403–415.

_____. *Discretio.* Les origenes patristiques et monastiques de la doctrine sur la prudence chez saint Thomas d'Aquin. Assen, 1967, Van Gorcum and Co.

Djuth, Marianne. *"Cassian's Use of the Figure Via Regia in Collatio II 'On Discretion.'"* SP 30, pp. 166–174. Leuven, Peeters, 1996.

Doyle, Leonard. *St. Benedict's Rule for Monasteries.* Collegeville, MN. The Liturgical Press, 1948.

Driscoll, Jeremy. *"The Psalms and Psychic Conversion,"* CS 22 (1987), 99–110.

_____. *"Listlessness in the Mirror for Monks of Evagrius Ponticus,"* CS 24 (1989), 206–214.

_____. *"Gentleness in the 'Ad Monachos' of Evagrius Ponticus,"* SM 32 (1990), 295–321.

_____. The *"Ad monachos"* of Evagrius Ponticus: Its Structure and a Select Commentary. SA 104. Rome, Pontificio Ateneo S. Anselmo, 1991.

_____. *"Penthos and Tears in Evagrius Ponticus."* SM 36 (1994), 147–164.

Driver, Steven D. *"From Palestinian Ignorance to Egyptian Wisdom: Cassian's Challenge to Jerome's Monastic Teaching."* ABR 48 (1997).

_____. *"The Reading of Egyptian Monastic Culture in John Cassian."* Ph.D. diss., University of Toronto, 1994.

Dublanche, E. *"Ascetisme,"* DTC, Tome I,2 (Paris, 1932), 2055–2077.

_____. *"Morale,"* DTC, Tome X, 2 (Paris, 1932), 2397–2458.

Ernetti, D. Pellegrino Maria. *S. Giovanni Cassiano: Istituzioni dei Cenobiti e rimedi contro gli vizi capitali.* Intro., trad., et annotazioni di D. Pellegrino Maria Ernetti, Monaco della Badia di Praglia. Vol. I (Scritti Monastici 20; Serie Ascetico-Mistico, 14). Tip. d. Prov. Patavina di S. Antonio dei Fr. M. Conv.; Padova, 1957.

Evagrius Ponticus. *De malignis cogitationibus (De mal. cog.).* PG 79:1200D–1233A, PG 40:1236C–1244B.

_____. *De octo spiritibus malitiae (De octo spir. mal.).* PG 79:1145A–1164D.

_____. *De oratione (De orat.).* PG 79:1165A–1200C.

_____. *Rerum monachalium rationes (Rerum mon. rat.).* PG 40:1252D–1264C.

_____. *Scholia in Proverbia (Schol. in Prov.).* Greek text and French trans. Paul Gehin. *Evagre le Pontique: Scholies aux Proverbes.* SC 340 (Paris, 1987).

_____. *De vitiis quae opposita sunt virtutibus (De vit.).* PG 79:1140B–1144D.

Evdokimov, Paul. *Les ages de la vie spirituelle des Peres du desert a nos jours,* Paris, 1965; trad. It.: *Le eta della vita spirituale,* Bologna, 1968.

Evelyn-White, Hugh Gerard. *The Monasteries of the Wâdi 'n Natrûn.* 3 vols. New York, Metro. Museum of Art, 1932–1933.

Festugière, Andre-Jean. Les moines d'Orient, 4 vols., Paris, 1961–1965.

_____. *Historia Monachorum in Aegypto,* Subsidia Hagiographica, no. 53, Bruxelles, 1971.

Fiske, Adele. "*Cassian and Monastic Friendship.*" ABR 12 (1961), 190–205.

Florensky, Pavel. *Le porte regali. Saggio sull'icona.* 2nd ed., Adelphi, Milano, 1981.

Frank, Karl Suso. "Johannes Cassian, *De institutis coenobiorum.* Normativer Erzähltext, präskriptiver Regeltext und appellative Du-Anrede." In *Dialogische Strukturen. Dialogic Structures. Festschrift für Willi Erzgräber,* pp. 7–16. Ed. Thomas Kuhn and Ursula Schaefer. Tübingen, Gunter Narr, 1996.

_____. "*John Cassian on John Cassian.*" SP 30 (1996), 418–433.

Frankenberg, Wilhelm. (Ed.) "Euagrius Pontikos." *Abhandlungen der königlichen Gesellschaft der Wissenschaften zu Göttingen, Phil.–Hist. Klasse,* N.F. XIII, 2 (Berlin, 1912). Syriac version with Greek text. In particular, *Capita cognoscitiva* (pp. 422–471), *Antirrheticos* (pp. 472–545), *Protrepticus* (pp. 554–556), and *Paraenetikos* (pp. 557–562).

Fry, Timothy. *The Rule of St. Benedict,* ed. (In Latin and English with Notes). Collegeville, MN: The Liturgical Press, 1981.

Gannon, T. & Traub, G. *The Desert and the City.* London: MacMillan Co., 1969.

Gargano, Guido Innocenzo. "*Cultura e Spiritualita nel Monachesimo Antico.*" SA 103, Rome, 1990.

_____. "*La 'Collatio XIV' di Giovanni Cassiano.*" Pontificio Ateneo Anselmiano, Roma, 1991.

Gazet, Alardus. *Commentarius from Cassiani Opera Omnia.* Douai, 1616. Reprinted in PL 49:55C–476C and 50:477A–1328D.

Giamberardini, G., & Gelsi, D. "*Scete.*" DIP 8: 1023–1030.

Gibson, Edgar C.S. "Prolegomena." *The Works of John Cassian*. NPNF, 2nd Series, Vol. 11, 1982.

Godet, P. "*Cassien*." DTC, Tome 2 (Paris, 1932), 1823–1829.

____. "*Evagre*." DTC, Tome 5 (Paris, 1939), 1611–1612.

Golinski, Z. "Doctrina Cassiani de mendacio officioso." *Collectanea Theologica* 17 (1936), 491–503.

Gómez, Alberto. "Compunctio lacrymarum. Doctrina de la compunción en el monacato latino de los siglos IV–VI." *Collectanea Ordinis Cisterciensium Reformatorum* 23 (1961), 232–253.

Gould, Grahm. *The Desert Fathers on Monastic Community*. Oxford Early Christian Studies. Oxford, Clarendon Press, 1993.

____. "The Image of God and the Anthropomorphite Controversy in Fourth Century Monasticism." In *Origeniana Quinta. Papers of the Fifth International Origen Congress*, Boston College, 14–18 August 1989, 549–557. Ed. Robert J. Daly. Bibliotheca Ephemeridum Theologicarum Lovaniensium 105. Leuven, University Press, 1992.

Greer, Rowan. *Origen*. trans. The Classics of Western Spirituality Series, New York, Paulist Press, 1979.

Gregg, R. C. *Athanasius, The Life of Antony and the Letter to Marcellinus*, Trans. & Intro., New York, 1980.

Gressmann, Hugo. (Ed.) "*Nonnenspiegel und Mönchsspiegel des Euagrios Pontikos*." TU 39, 4 (1913), 143–165; in particular, *Ad monachos* and *Ad virgines*.

Gribomont, Jean. "*Evagrio Pontico*." DP 1: 1313–1314.

____. Guillaumont, A., Špidlík, T., & de Vogüé, A. "*Preghiera*." DIP 7 (1983), 582–606.

____. "The Commentaries of Adalbert de Vogüé and the Great Monastic Tradition." ABR 36 (1985), 229–252. Trans. Terrence Kardong from "Les commentaires d'Adalbert de Vogüé et la grande tradition monastique." In *Commentaria in S. Regulam* I, 109–143. SA 84. Rome, 1982.

Griffe, Élie. "Cassien a-t-il été prêtre d'Antioche?" *Bulletin de littérature ecclésiastique* 55 (1954), 240–244.

Guibert, Joseph de. "*La componction du coeur*." RAM 15 (1934), 225–240.

____. *The Theology of the Spiritual Life*. Trans. by Paul Barrett, New York, Sheed & Ward, 1953.

Guillaumont, Antoine. *Les six Centuries des "Képhalaia Gnostica" d'Évagre le Pontique*. Edition de la version syriaque commune et edition d'une nouvelle version syriaque, integrale, avec une double traduction francaise; Graffin-Nau, PO 28, fasc. 1, no. 134, Paris, 1958.

____. "*Évagre et les anathématismes antiorigénistes de 553*." TU 78 (1961), 219–226.

____. Ed. "*Les 'Képhalaia Gnostica' d'Évagre le Pontique et l'histoire de l'origénisme chez les Grecs et chez les Syriens*." Patristica Sorboniensia 5, Paris, 1962.

_____. *"Une inscription copte sur la 'Prière de Jésus.'"* OCP 34 (1968), 310–325.

_____. *"Un philosophe au désert: Évagre le Pontique."* RHR 181 (1972), 29–56.

_____. *"La prière de Jésus chez les moines d'Égypte."* ECR 6 (1974), 66–71.

_____. "Le problème des deux Macaire dans les Apophthegmata Patrum." *Irénikon* 48 (1975), 41–59.

_____. *"La conception du désert chez les moines d'Égypte."* RHR 188 (1975), 3–21.

_____. "Les visions mystiques dans le *monachisme* oriental chrétien," in *Colloque organisé par le Secrétariat d'Etat à la Culture*, 116–127, Paris, 1976.

_____. "Histoire des moines aux Kellia," *Orientalia Lovaniensia Periodica* 8 (1977), 187–203.

_____. *Aux origines du monachisme chrétien: Pour une phénoménologie du monachisme*. Spiritualité Orientale, no. 30, Bellefontaine, 1979.

_____. "Evagrius Ponticus." TRE 10 (1982), 565–570.

_____. *"La 'preghiera pura' die Evagrio e l'influsso del Neoplatonismo."* DIP 7 (1983), 591–595.

_____. *"Demon, 2. Évagre le Pontique."* DSAM 3: 196–205.

_____. *"Le 'coeur' chez les spirituels grecs à l'époque ancienne."* DSAM 2: 2281–2288.

Guillaumont, Antoine & Claire. *"Le texte véritable des 'Gnostica' d'Évagre le Pontique."* RHR 142 (1952), 156–205.

_____. *"Demon dans la plus ancienne litterature monastique."* DSAM 3 (1957), 189–212.

_____. *"Évagre le Pontique."* DSAM 4,2 (1961), 1731–1744.

_____. *Évagre le Pontique: Traité Pratique ou Le Moine*. Tome 1, SC 170 (1971).

_____. "Evagrius Ponticus." *Reallexikon für Antike und Christentum* 6: 1088–1107.

_____. Eds. *Évagre le Pontique. Le Gnostique ou a celui qui est devenu digne de la science*. SC 356 (1989).

Guy, Jean-Claude. *"Remarques sur le texte des Apophthegmata Patrum."* RSR 43 (1955), 252–258.

_____. *"Note sur l'évolution du genre apophthegmatique."* RAM 32 (1956), 63–68.

_____. *"Un dialogue monastique inédit."* RAM 33 (1957), 171–188.

_____. *"Écriture Sainte et vie spirituelle."* DSAM 4, 1 (1960), 159–164.

_____. *Jean Cassien: Vie et doctrine spirituelle*. Lethielleux, Editeur, 10 Rue Cassette, Paris, 1961.

_____. "Les Apophthegmata Patrum," *Théologie de la vie monastique* (Études sur la Tradition patristique), Théologie, 49, Paris, Aubien, 1961, pp. 73–83.

_____. *"Le Centre monastique de Scété dans la littérature du V siècle."* OCP 30, 1 (1964), 129–147.

____. *Jean Cassien. Institutions cénobitiques.* SC 109 (1965).

____. *"La place du* contemptus mundi *dans le monachisme ancien."* RAM 41 (1965), 245–248.

____. *"Jean Cassien, historien du monashisme égyptien?"* SP 8 [TU 93 (1966)], 363–372.

____. *"Educational Innovation in the Desert Fathers."* ECR 6 (1974), 44–51.

____. *Recherches sur la tradition grecque des Apophthegmata Patrum.* 2nd ed. Subsidia hagiographica 36. Societe des Bollandistes, Brussels, 1984.

____. *Les Apophthegmes des Pères. Collection systématique.* SC 387 (1993).

____. *"Cassian, Saint John."* CE, 461–464.

Haag, Modestus. *"A Precarious Balance: Flesh and Spirit in Cassian's Works."* ABR 19 (1968), 180–192.

Hassett, Maurice. "John Cassian." *The Catholic Encyclopedia*, Vol. 3. New York: Appleton Co., 1908, pp. 404–405.

Hausherr, Irénée. *La méthode d'oraison hésychaste.* OC 9:2, no.36 (1927).

____. *"Par delà l'oraison pure grâce à une coquille. A propos d'un texte d'Évagre."* RAM 13 (1932), 184–188.

____. *"L'origine de la théorie orientale des huit péchés capitaux."* OCA 30 (1933), 164–175.

____. *"Centuries."* DSAM 2: 416–418.

____. *"Contemplation. Évagre le Pontique."* DSAM 2: 1775–1785.

____. *"Le Traité de l'oraison d'Évagre le Pontique (Pseudo-Nil)."* RAM 15 (1934), 34–93, 113–170.

____. *"Les grands courants de la spiritualité orientale."* OCP 1 (1935), 114–138.

____. *"Ignorance infinie."* OCP 2 (1936), 351–362.

____. *"Nouveaux fragments grecs d'Évagre le Pontique."* OCP 5 (1939), 229–233.

____. *"Le 'de Oratione d'Évagre le Pontique in Syriaque et en Arabe."* OCP 5 (1939), 7–71.

____. *"Les Orientaux connaissent-ils les 'nuits' de saint Jean de la Croix?"* OCP 12 (1946), 5–46.

____. *"Opus Dei."* OCP 13 (1947), 195–218; also, MS 11 (1975), 181–204 and OCA 183 (1969), 121–144.

____. *"Contemplation chez les Grecs et autres orientaux chretiens."* DSAM 2 (1953): 1762–1872 (sous le nom de J. Lemaitre).

____. *"Les Exercises Spirituels de Saint Ignace et la methode d'oraison hesychastique."* OCP 20 (1954), 7–26.

____. *"Comment, priaient les Pères."* RAM 32 (1956), 33–58, 284–296.

____. *"Spiritualite Monacale et Unite Chretienne."* OCA 153 (1958), 15–32.

____. *"Ignorance infinie ou science infinie?"* OCP 25 (1959), 44–52.

____. *Les lecons d'un contemplatif. Le Traité de l'oraison d'Évagre le Pontique.* Paris, Beauchesne, 1960.

____. *Hésychasme et prière.* OCA 176 (1966); in particular, *"La prière perpétuelle du chrétien,"* pp. 255–303.

_____. *Penthos: The Doctrine of Compunction in the Christian East.* CSS 53. Kalamazoo, Cistercian, 1982. Also, OCA 132 (1944).

_____. *Spiritual Direction in the Early Christian East.* CSS 116. Kalamazoo, Cistercian, 1990. Also, OCA 144 (1955).

Heussi, Karl. *Der Ursprung des Mönchtums.* Tübingen, 1936.

Hoch, Alexander. *Lehre des Johannes Cassianus von Natur und Gnade: Ein Beitrag zur Geschichte des Gnadenstreits im 5. Jahrhundert.* Freiburg im Breisgau: Herder, 1895.

_____. "Zur Heimat des Johannes Cassianus." *Theologisches Quartalschrift* 82 (1900), 43–69.

Holze, Heinrich. *Erfahrung und Theologie im frühen Mönchtum. Untersuchungen zu einer Theologie des monastischen Lebens bei den ägyptischen Mönchsvatern, Johannes Cassian und Benedikt von Nursia.* Forschungen zur Kirchen- und Dogmengeschichte 48. Göttingen: Vanderhoeck und Ruprecht, 1992.

Honselmann, Klemens. "Bruchstücke von Auszügen aus Werken Cassians– Reste einer verlorenen Schrift des Eucherius von Lyon?" *Theologie und Glaube* 51 (1961), 300–304.

Jennett, Michael James. *A Descriptive Presentation on John Cassian and his Treatise on Prayer: The Relationship of Virtue and Prayer.* Dissertation ad Lauream in Facultate S. Theologiae Apud Pontificiam Universitatem S. Thomae de Urbe, Rome, 1981.

Jetté, Fernand. "*Etat.*" DSAM 4, 2 (1961): 1372–1388.

Joest, Christoph. "*Die Bedeutung von Akedia und Apatheia bei Evagrios Pontikos.*" SM 35 (1993), 7–53.

Kadloubovsky, E. & Palmer, G.E.H. *Writings from the Philokalia on Prayer of the Heart.* Translation, Faber & Faber, London, 1979.

_____. *Early Fathers from the Philokalia.* Translation, Faber & Faber, London, 1981.

Kardong, Terrence. "*John Cassian's Teaching on Perfect Chastity.*" ABR 30 (1979), 249–263.

_____. "Aiming at the Mark: Cassian's Metaphor for the Monastic Quest." CS 22 (1987), 213–221.

_____. "*Benedict's Use of Cassianic Formulae for Spiritual Progress.*" SM 34 (1992), 233–252.

_____. "*John Cassian's Evaluation of Monastic Practices.*" ABR 43 (1992), 82–105.

_____. *Benedict's Rule: A Translation and Commentary.* Collegeville, MN, Liturgical Press, 1996.

Kasper, Clemens. *Theologie und Askese: Die spiritualität des Inselmönchtums von Lérins im 5. Jahrhundert. Beiträge zur Geschichte des Alten Mönchtums und das Benediktinertums 40.* Münster, Aschendorff, 1991.

Keating, Thomas Aquinas. "*The Two Streams of Cenobitic Tradition in the Rule of St. Benedict.*" CS 11, 4 (1976), 257–268.

Kline, Francis. *"The Christology of Evagrius and the Parent System of Origen."* CS 20 (1985), 155–183.

Leclercq, Henri. *"Marseille."* DACL 10: 2204–2293.

Leroy, Julien. *"Le cénobitisme chez Cassien."* RAM 43 (1967), 121–158.

_____. *"Les préfaces des écrits monastiques de Jean Cassien."* RAM 42 (1966), 157–180.

Leturia, Pedro de. *"El influjo de San Onofre in San Ignacio a base de un texto inédito de Nadal."* Manresa II (1926), 224–238.

Levko, John. *"Incessant Prayer and John Cassian."* Dk 28, 2 (1995), 71–90.

_____. *"Patience in a Life of Prayer for John Cassian."* Dk 28, 3 (1995), 167–172.

_____. *"Temptation and Its Relationship to Prayer for John Cassian."* Dk 29, 2 (1996), 85–94.

_____. *"Self-control in a Life of Prayer for John Cassian."* Dk 29, 2 (1996), 142–154.

_____. *"The Relationship of Prayer to Discretion and Spiritual Direction for John Cassian."* SVTQ 40, 3 (1996), 155–171.

_____. *"Inside Prayer with John Cassian."* Dk 30, 2–3 (1997), 165–173.

_____. *"The Spiritual Journey from Lukewarmness to Steadfastness for John Cassian."* Dk 31, 1 (1998), 5–13.

_____. *"Prison: School of Prayer?"* Dk 35,2 (2002), 105–112.

Leyser, Conrad. *"Lectio divina, oratio pura: Rhetoric and the Techniques of Asceticism in the 'Conferences' of John Cassian."* In *Modelli di santità e modelli di comportamento: contrasti, intersezioni, complementarità*, pp. 79–105. Ed. Giulia Barone, Marina Caffiero and Francesco Scorza Barcellona. Turin, Rosenberg e Sellier, 1994.

Lienhard, Joseph T. *Paulinus of Nola and Early Western Monasticism.* With a study of the chronology of his works and an annotated bibliography, 1879–1976, Koln-Bonn, 1977, Peter Hanstein Verlag.

_____. *"On 'Discernment of Spirits' in the Early Church."* TS 41,3 (1980), 505–529.

Loorits, Oskar. *Der Heilige Kassian und die Schaltjahrlegende.* Folklore Fellows Communications 149. Helsinki, Suomalainen Tiedeakatemia, 1954.

Lorié, L. Th.A. *Spiritual terminology in the Latin translation of the Vita Antonii with reference to fourth and fifth century monastic literature.* Latinitas Christianorum Primaeva, xi, Nymegen, 1955.

Lossky, Vladimir. *A l'image et à la ressemblance de Dieu.* Paris, 1967.

_____. *The Mystical Theology of the Eastern Church.* New York: St. Vladimir's Seminary Press, 1976.

_____. *The Vision of God.* New York: St. Vladimir's Seminary Press, 1983.

Lot-Borodine, Myrrha. *"Le mystère du 'don des larmes' dans l'Orient chrétien."* Supplément à la Vie Spirituelle (September 1936), 65–110.

Louf, Andre. *The Message of Monastic Spirituality.* Desclee Co., Inc., 1964.

_____. *"L'acédie chez Évagre le Pontique."* Concilium 99 (1974), 113–117.

Luibheid, Colm. *John Cassian: Conferences*, trans. & pref. by Colm Luibheid, intro. by Owen Chadwick, Paulist Press, New York, 1985.

Mackean, W.H. *Christian Monasticism in Egypt to the close of the fourth century*. Studies in Church History, 1920.

Macqueen, D.J. *"John Cassian on Grace and Free Will, with Particular Reference to Institutio XII and Collatio XIII."* RTAM 44 (1977), 5–28.

Main, Dom John. *"Prayer in the Tradition of John Cassian."* CS 12 (1977), 184–190, 272–281.

Malone, Edward E. *"The Monk and the Martyr."* SA 38 (1956), 201–228.

Maloney George. *The Cosmic Christ*. Sheed & Ward, New York, 1967.

____. *Russian Hesychasm*. The Spirituality of Nil Sorskij. Mouton, The Hague-Paris, 1973.

____. *Prayer of the Heart*. Ave Maria Press, 1981.

Marrou, Henri I. "Jean Cassien à Marseille." *Revue du moyen age latin* 1 (1945), 5–26.

____. *"La patrie de Jean Cassien."* OCP 13 (1947), 588–596.

____. "Le fondateur de Saint-Victor a Marseille: Jean Cassien." *Provence historique* 16 (1966), 297–308.

Marsili, Salvatore. *Giovanni Cassiano ed Evagrio Pontico*. SA 5 (1936).

Marx, Michael. *Incessant Prayer in Ancient Monastic Literature*. Rome, Facultas Theologica Sancti Anselmi de Urbe, 1946.

McGuire, Brian P. *Friendship and Community: the Monastic Experience, 350–1250*. CSS 95 (1988).

Ménager, A. "La patrie de Cassien." *Échos d'Orient* 21 (1921), 330–358.

____. *"Cassien et Clément d'Alexandrie."* VS 9 (1924), 138–152.

Mensbrugghe, A. van der. *"Prayer-time in Egyptian monasticism (320–450)."* SP 2 [TU 64, Berlin] (1957), 435–454.

Merton, Thomas. *The Wisdom of the Desert*. New York, New Directions Book, 1961.

____. *"The Spiritual Father in the Desert Tradition."* MS 5 (1968).

____. *Contemplative Prayer*. Garden City, New York: Image Books, 1971.

____. *The Climate of Monastic Prayer*. CSS 1 (1973).

Meyer, Robert. *Palladius: The Lausiac History*. ACW 34 (1965).

____. *"Palladius and the Study of Scripture."* SP 13 (1975), 487–490.

Miguel, Pierre. *"Un homme d'expérience: Cassien."* CC 30 (1968), 131–146.

____. *Lexique du desert. Étude de quelques mots-clés du vocabulaire monastique grec ancien*. Spiritualité orientale 44. Bégrolles-en-Mauges, Abbaye de Bellefontaine, 1986.

Monchanin, Jules. *"Yoga and Hesychasm."* CS 10, 2 (1975), 85–92.

Mortari, L. *Vita e Detti dei Padri del Deserto*. Rome, 1975.

Munz, Peter. *"John Cassian."* JEH 11 (1960), 1–22.

Murphy, F.X. *"Jesus Prayer."* NCE 7 (1967), 971.

____. *"Hesychasm."* NCE 6 (1967), 1089–1090.

____. "Evagrius Ponticus and Origenism." *Origeniana Tertia*, ed. by R.P.C. Hanson and H. Crouzel, 253–269, Rome, 1985.

Musurillo, Herbert. "The Problem of Ascetical Fasting in the Greek Patristic Tradition." *Traditio* 12 (1956), 1–64.

Neuhausen, Karl A. "Zu Cassians Traktat De amicitia (Coll. 16)." *Studien zur Literatur der Spätantike*, pp. 181–218. Ed. C. Gnilka and W. Schetter. Antiquitas, Reihe 1, Band 23. Bonn, Habelt, 1975.

O'Laughlin, Michael. "*Origenism in the Desert. Anthropology and Integration in Evagrius Ponticus.*" Th.D. diss., Harvard University, 1987.

_____. "*The Bible, the Demons and the Desert: Evaluating the Antirrheticus of Evagrius Ponticus.*" SM 34 (1992), 201–215.

Olphe-Galliard, Michel. "*Vie contemplative et vie active d'après Cassien.*" RAM 16 (1935), 252–288.

_____. "*Les sources de la Conférence XI de Cassien.*" RAM 16 (1935), 289–298.

_____. "*Debat a propos de Cassien.*" RAM 17 (1936), 181–191.

_____. "*La pureté de coeur d'après Cassien.*" RAM 17 (1936), 28–60.

_____. "*La science spirituelle d'après Cassien.*" RAM 18 (1937), 141–160.

_____. "*Cassien.*" DSAM 2 (1953), 214–276.

O'Meara, John. *Origen: Prayer—Exhortation to Martyrdom*. ACW 19 (1954).

Origen. *Philocalia*. Ed., French trans., and notes by Marguerite Harl. *Origène: Philocalie 1–20 Sur les Écritures*. SC 302 (Paris, 1983).

_____. *De oratione*. PG 11: 415–562.

_____. *De principiis (De princ.)*. Ed. P. Koetschau. GCS *Origenes Werke* 5 (Leipzig, 1913).

Palmer, G., Sherrard, P., Ware, K. *The Philokalia*, Vol. 1, translation, Faber & Faber, London, 1979.

Parente, Pascal. *The Ascetical Life*. St. Louis: B. Herder Book Co., 1945.

Paucker, C. von. "Die Latinität des Johannes Cassianus." *Romanische Forschungen* 2 (1886), 391–448.

Pegon, Joseph. "*Componction.*" DSAM 2:1312–1321.

Peifer, Claude. *Monastic Spirituality*. New York: Sheed and Ward, 1966.

Pelikan, Jaroslav. *The Christian Tradition: A History of the Development of Doctrine*. Vol. 1 (The Emergence of the Catholic Tradition 100–600), Chicago: The University of Chicago Press, 1971.

Pichery, Eugène. *Jean Cassien: Conférences*. SC 42,54, 64. Paris (1955–1959).

Placa, Alan & Riordan, Brendan. *Desert Silence: A Way of Prayer for an Unquiet Age*. Locust Valley, New York: Living Flame Press, 1978.

Plagnieux, Jean. "*Le grief de complicité entre erreurs nestorienne et pélagienne d'Augustin à Cassien par Prosper d'Aquitaine?*" REA 2 (1956), 391–402.

Poulain, Augustin. *The Graces of Interior Prayer*. Translated by Leonora Yorke Smith. St. Louis: B. Herder Book Co., 1950; see *Des grâces d'oraison*, 10th ed, Paris, Beauchesne, 1922.

Pozdiejevsky, F. *Les conceptions ascetiques de S. Jean Cassien* (Asketicskaja vozrenija prepodobnago Joanna Kassiana Rimljanina [presvitera massilijskago], 1902), Kazan, 1902.

Pricoco, Salvatore. *L'isola dei santi: Il cenobio di Lerino e le origini del monachesimo gallico*. Rome, Edizioni dell'Ateneo and Bizzarri, 1978.

Priestley, Gail Marie. *"Some Jungian Parallels to the Sayings of the Desert Fathers."* CS 11, 2 (1976), 102–123.

Pristas, Lauren. *"The Theological Anthropology of John Cassian."* Ph.D. diss., Boston College, 1993.

Quasten, Johannes. *Patrology*. 3 vols. Westminster, MD, Newman Press, 1950–1960.

Raasch, Juana. *"The Monastic Concept of Purity of Heart and Its Sources."* SM 8 (1966), 7–33, 183–213; 10 (1968), 7–55; 11 (1969), 269–314; 12 (1970), 7–41.

Rader, Rosemary. *Breaking Boundaries: Male/Female Friendship in Early Christian Communities*. Ramsey, NJ, Paulist Press, 1983.

Rahner, Hugo. *"Ignatius und die aszetische Tradition."* ZAM 17 (1942), 66–72.

Rahner, Karl. *"Le début d'une doctrine des cinq sens spirituels."* RAM 13 (1932), 113–145.

Ramsey, Boniface. "John Cassian: Student of Augustine." *Cistercian Studies Quarterly* 28 (1993), 5–15.

_____. *John Cassian. The Conferences*, English trans. & commentary. ACW 57 (1997).

_____. *John Cassian. The Institutes, translated & annotated*, ACW 58 (2000).

Rébillard, Eric. *"Quasi funambuli: Cassien et la controverse pélagienne sur la perfection."* REA 40 (1994), 197–210.

Refoulé, F. *"Rêves et vie spirituelle d'après Évagre le Pontique."* VS, supplement, 56 (1961), 470–516.

_____. *"La Christologie d'Évagre et l'Origénisme."* OCP 27 (1961), 221–266.

_____. *"La mystique d'Évagre et l'Origénisme."* VS, supplement, 64 (1963), 453–472.

_____. *"Evagrius Ponticus."* NCE 5 (1967), 644–645.

Régamey, P. *"La componction du coeur."* VS, supplement, 44 (1935), 1–16, 65–83; 45 (1935), 8–21, 86–99.

Regnault, Lucien. "La prière continuelle 'monologistos' dans la littérature apophthegmatique." *Irénikon* 47 (1974), 467–493.

_____. *"The Beatitudes in the Apophthegmata Patrum."* ECR 6 (1974), 22–43.

_____. "La prière de Jésus dans quelques apophtegmes conservés en arabe." *Irénikon* 52 (1979), 344–355.

Regula Cassiani. Ed. Henri Ledoyen. RB 94 (1984), 170–194.

Regula Magistri (Reg. Mag.). Ed and French trans. Adalbert de Vogüé. *La Règle du Maître*. SC 105–107 (Paris, 1964–1965).

Reitzenstein, Richard. *Historia Monachorum und Historia Lausiaca: Eine Studie zur Geschichte des Mönchtums und der frühchristlichen Begriffe Gnostiker und Pneumatiker*. Göttingen, Vandenhoeck und Ruprecht, 1916.

Roberts, Augustine. *"Spiritual Methods in Benedictine Life, Yesderday and Today."* CS 10, 3–4 (1975), 207–233.

Rodríguez, Alphonsus. *Practice of Perfection and Christian Virtues*. 3 vols., trans. by Joseph Richaby. Chicago: Loyola University Press, 1929.

Rondeau, M. J. *"Le commentaire sur les Psaumes d'Évagre le Pontique."* OCP 26 (1960), 307–348.

Ross, Maggie. *The Fountain and the Furnace: The Way of Tears and Fire*. New York, Paulist Press, 1987. See also "Tears and fire: recovering a neglected tradition." *Sobornost* 9, 1 (1987), 14–23.

Rousseau, Philip. *"Cassian, Contemplation and the Coenobitic Life."* JEH 26 (1975), 113–126.

_____. *Ascetics, Authority, and the Church in the Age of Jerome and Cassian*. Oxford Historical Monographs. Oxford, Oxford University Press, 1978.

_____. "Cassian: Monastery and World." In *The Certainty of Doubt. Tributes to Peter Munz*, pp. 68–89. Ed. Miles Fairburn and W. H. Oliver. Wellington, New Zealand, Victoria University Press, 1995.

Russell, Kenneth C. *"John Cassian on a Delicate Subject."* CS 27 (1992), 1–12.

Ryan, Edward J. *"The Invocation of the Divine Name in Sinaite Spirituality."* ECQ 14, 4 (1961–1962), 241–249.

Ryan, Granger & Ripperger, Helmut. *The Golden Legend of Jacobus de Voragine*. Trans. & adapted from the Latin. Longmans, Green & Co., New York, 1941.

Ryan, Patrick. *"Two Monastic Treatises."* CS 12, 3 (1977), 212–224.

Salles, M. *"La doctrine spirituelle de Cassien."* These (inedite), Institut Catholique de Toulouse, 1929.

Saudreau, Auguste. *"Le Spiritualite d'Évagre le Pontique."* VS, supplement, (1936), 180–190.

Schaff, Philip & Wace, Henry. *"Sulpitius Severus, Vincent of Lerins, John Cassian: Church Histories."* Ed. NPNF, 2nd series, vol. 11, New York: Wm. B. Eerdmans Pub. Co., 1982 (reprinted).

Sheridan, Mark. *Concordanza elettronica alle opere de Giovanni Cassiano*. Rome, 1990.

_____. "Models and Images of Spiritual Progress in the Works of John Cassian." In *Spiritual Progress: Studies in the Spirituality of Late Antiquity and Early Monasticism. Papers of the Symposium of the Monastic Institute* Rome, Pontificio Ateneo Sant' Anselmo 14–15 May 1992, pp. 101–125. Ed. Jeremy Driscoll & Mark Sheridan. SA 115 (1994).

Solignac, Aimé. *"Semipélagiens."* DSAM 14: 556–568.

_____. *"Victor de Vita."* DSAM 16: 547–552.

_____. *"Vie active, vie contemplative, vie mixte."* DSAM 16: 592–623.

Sophrony, Archimandrite. *"De la nécessité des trois renoncements chez St. Cassien le Romain et St. Jean Climaque."* SP 5 (TU 80) 393–400. Berlin, Akademie Verlag, 1962.

_____. "Principles of Orthodox Asceticism" in *The Orthodox Ethos: Studies in Orthodoxy*, vol. 1, ed. by A. J. Philippou, Holywell Press, Oxford, 1964, pp. 259–286.

Špidlík, Tomáš. *La doctrine spirituelle de Theophane le Reclus*. OCA 172 (1965).

———. *"Bizantino, monachesimo."* DIP 1 (1973), 1466–1474.

———. "La direzione spirituale nell'Oriente cristiano." *Vita consacrata* 16 (1980), 502–514, 573–582.

———. *Ignazio di Loyola e la Spiritualità Orientale.* Guida alla lettura degli Esercizi. Edizioni Studium, Roma, 1994.

Spinelli. "Teologia e 'teoria' nella Conlatio de Protectione Dei di Giovanni Cassiano." *Benedictina* 31 (1984), 23–35.

Sternberg, Thomas. "Der vermeintliche Ursprung der westlichen Diakonien in Ägypten und die Conlationes des Johannes Cassian." *Jahrbuch für Antike und Christentum* 31 (1988), 173–209.

Stewart, Columba. *"John Cassian on Unceasing Prayer."* MS 15 (1984), 159–177.

———. "The Desert Fathers on Radical Honesty about the Self." *Sobornost* 12 (1990), 25–39, 131–156.

———. *Cassian the Monk.* Oxford University Press, 1998.

Summa, Gerd. *Geistliche Unterscheidung bei Johannes Cassian.* Studien zur systematischen und spirituellen Theologie 7. Würzburg, Echter, 1992.

Taft, Robert. "Praise in the Desert: The Coptic Monastic Office Yesterday and Today." *Worship* 56 (1982), 513–536.

———. *The Liturgy of the Hours in East and West: The Origins of the Divine Office and Its Meaning for Today.* Collegeville, MN, Liturgical Press, 1986.

Tibiletti, Carlo. "Giovanni Cassiano. Formazione e dottrina." *Augustinianum* 17 (1977), 355–380.

Tugwell, Simon. *Prayer: Living With God.* 2 vols. Dublin: Veritas Publications, 1975.

———. *Evagrius Ponticus: Praktikos & On Prayer.* Trans. Published privately by the Faculty of Theology, Oxford, 1987.

Tunink, Wilfrid. *"The Apostolic Life."* ABR 14 (1963), 516–530.

Turner, H.J.M. *"Evagrius Ponticus, Teacher of Prayer."* ECR 7: 145–148.

Vannier, Marie-Anne. *"Jean Cassien a-t-il fait oeuvre de théologien dans le De incarnatione domini?"* RSR 66 (1992), 119–131.

———. "L'influence de Jean Chrysostome sur l'argumentation scripturaire du De Incarnatione de Jean Cassien." RSR 69 (1995), 453–462.

Veilleux, Armand. *La liturgie dans le cénobitisme pachômien en quatrième siècle.* SA 57 (1968), 228–235.

———. *Pachomian Koinonia.* 3 vols. CSS 45–47 (1980–1982).

Viller, Marcel. *"Le Martyre et l'ascese."* RAM 6 (1925), 105–142.

———. *"Aux sources de la spiritualité de saint Maxime."* RAM 11 (1930), 156–184, 239–268, 331–336.

——— & Rahner, Karl. *Aszese und Mystik in der Vaterzeit.* Freiburg im Breisgau, Herder, 1939.

Vogüé, Adalbert de. "Monachisme et Église dans la pensée de Cassien." In *Théologie de la vie monastique: Études sur la Tradition patristique*, pp. 213–240. Théologie 49. Paris, Aubier, 1961.

_____. *"Prayer in the Rule of St. Benedict."* MS 7 (1969), 113–140.

_____. *"Sub regula vel abbate."* In Rule and Life: An Interdisciplinary Symposium, pp. 21–64. CSS 12. Ed. M. Basil Pennington. Spencer, Mass. Cistercian Pub., 1971.

_____. *"To Study the Early Monks."* CC 37 (1975), 93–113.

_____. *"Les deux fonctions de la méditation dans les Règles monastiques anciennes."* RHS 51 (1975), 3–16.

_____. *"The Cenobitic Rules of the West."* CS 12, 3 (1977), 175–183.

_____. *"Les mentions des oeuvres de Cassien chez Saint Benoît et ses contemporains."* SM 20 (1978), 275–285.

_____. *"Pour comprendre Cassien. Un survol des Conférences."* CC 39 (1979), 250–272.

_____. *"Prayer in Early Western Monasticism."* WS 3 (1981), 106–120.

_____. *"De Cassien au Maître et à Eugippe: le titre du chapitre de l'humilité."* SM 23 (1981), 247–261.

_____. *Les Règles des saint Pères.* SC 297–298. Paris, Cerf, 1982.

_____. *"Une interpolation inspirée de Cassien dans un texte monastique de Césaire d'Arles."* SM 25 (1983), 217–221.

_____. *The Rule of Saint Benedict, a Doctrinal and Spiritual Commentary.* CSS 54 Kalamazoo, Cistercian Pub., 1983.

_____. *"La lecture du Matin dans les Sentences d'Evagre et le De Virginitate attribue a saint Athanase."* SM 26 (1984), 7–11.

_____. *"Understanding Cassian: A Survey of the Conferences."* CS 19 (1984), 101–121.

_____. *"Twenty-Five Years of Benedictine Hermeneutics—An Examination of Conscience."* ABR 36 (1985), 402–452.

_____. *"Un morceau célèbre de Cassien parmi des extraits d'Évagre."* SM 27 (1985), 7–12.

_____. *"La `Regula Cassiani': sa destination et ses rapports avec le monachisme fructuosien."* RB 95 (1985), 185–231.

_____. *"Les sources des quatre premiers livres des Institutions de Jean Cassien. Introduction aux recherches sur les anciennes règles monastiques latines."* SM 27 (1985), 241–311.

_____. *"Les débuts de la vie monastique à Lérins. Remarques sur un ouvrage récent."* RHR 88 (1993), 5–53.

Vogüé, Adalbert de and Neufville, Jean. *La Règle de Saint Benoît.* 7 vols. SC 181–186, 186a (Paris, 1971–1977).

Völker, Walther. *Der wahre Gnostiker nach Clemens Alexandrinus.* Berlin, Akademie-Verlag, 1952.

Vööbus, Arthur. *History of Asceticism in the Syrian Orient.* Early Monasticism in Mesopotamia and Syria. Vol. 2, Louvain, Secretariat Du Corpus SCO, 1960.

Vuillaume, Christophe. *"Le jeûne dans la tradition monastique ancienne et aujourd'hui."* CC 51 (1989), 42–78.

Waddell, Helen. *The Desert Fathers.* Ann Arbor, University of Michigan Press, 1957.

Walsh, James. "The Discernment of Spirits." *The Way*, supplement, 16 (1972), 54–66.

Ward, Benedicta. *Harlots of the Desert: A Study of Repentance in Early Monastic Sources.* London, Mowbray, 1987.

_____. *The Sayings of the Desert Fathers.* The Alphabetical Collection. Trans. with foreword by B. Ward. Preface by Metr. Anthony of Sourozh. CSS 59, Kalamazoo, Mich., 1984.

_____. *The Wisdom of the Desert Fathers.* Apophthegmata Patrum from the Anonymous Series. Trans. with intro. by B. Ward. Forward by Metr. Anthony Bloom. SLG Press, Convent of the Incarnation, Fairacres, Oxford, 1975.

_____, & Norman, Russell. *The Lives of the Desert Fathers.* The Historia Monachorum in Aegypto. Trans. by N. Russell. Intro. by B. Ward. CSS 34, Kalamazoo, Mich., 1980.

Ware, Kallistos. *"Pray Without Ceasing: The Ideal of Continual Prayer in Eastern Monasticism."* ECR 2 (1969), 253–261.

Wathen, Ambrose. *Silence.* CSS 22 (1973).

Weber, Hans-Oskar. *Die Stellung des Johannes Cassianus zur ausserpachomianischen Mönchstradition.* Münster, Aschendorff, 1961.

Weisheipl, James. "Cassianus, Johannes." *Encyclopedia Americana* 5 (1972), 769.

Wenzel, S. *The Sin of Sloth: Acedia in Medieval Thought and Literature.* Chapel Hill, 1967.

Widmann, J. "Discretio." *Studien und Mitteilungen zur Geschichte des Benediktiner—Ordens und seiner Zweige.* Munchen, 58 (1940), 21–28.

Wrzol, Ludwig. "Die Psychologie des Johannes Cassianus." *Divus Thomas* 32 (1918), 181–213, 425–456; 34 (1920), 70–96; 36 (1922), 269–294.

Wulf, Friedrich. *"Priestertum und Ratestand (II)."* GL 33 (1960), 247–261.

_____. "Ascese." *Encyclopédie de la Foi* (sous la direction de H. Fries, Paris) 1 (1967), 128–137.

_____. *Ignatius of Loyola, His Personality and Spiritual Heritage, 1556–1956.* Ed. by F. Wulf., The Institute of Jesuit Sources, St. Louis, 1977.

SELECT INDEX